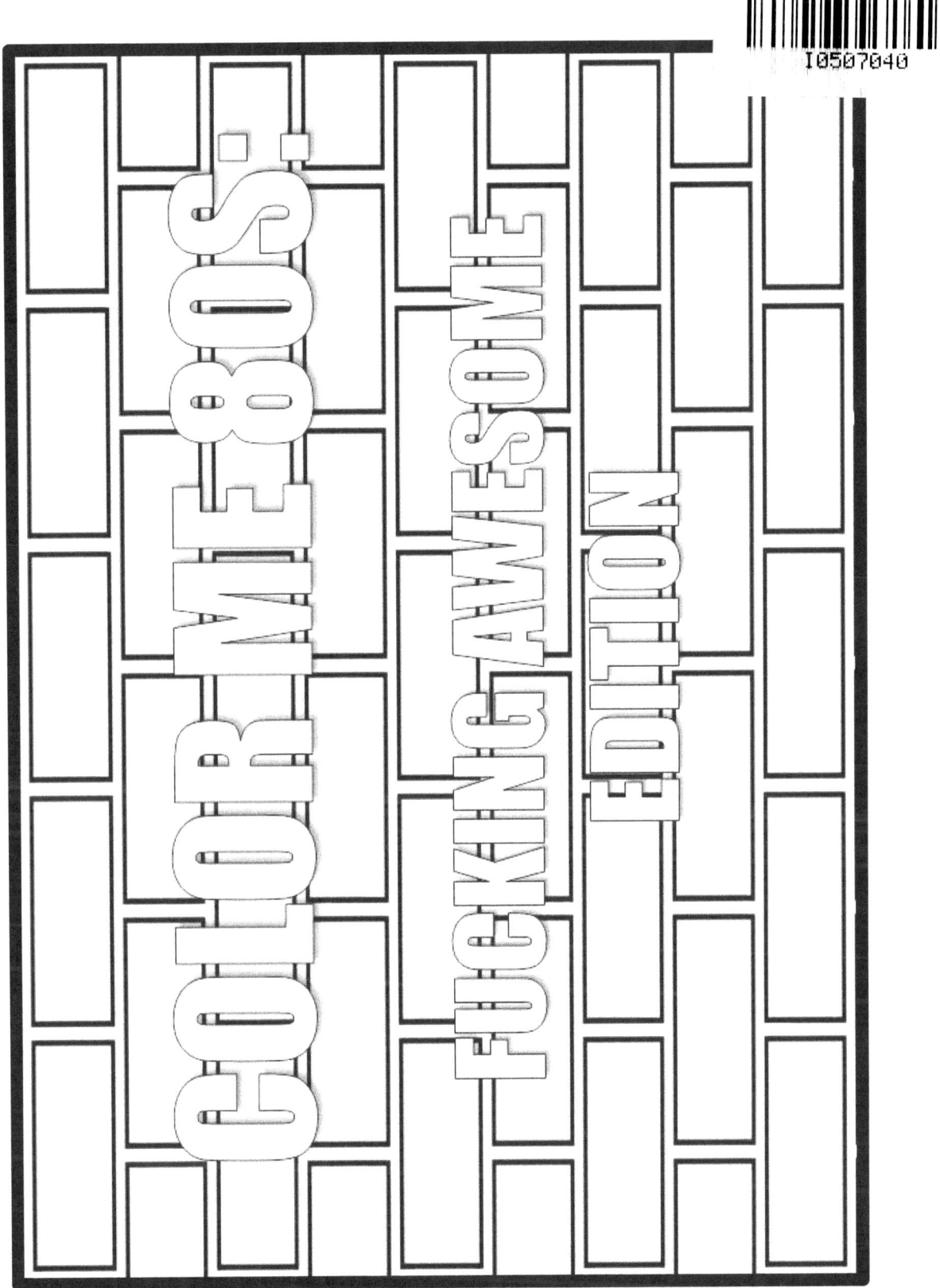

ISBN 9798620039937

Copyright 2020 by Laura Quinn

Worldwide Electronic & Digital Rights

Worldwide English Language Print Rights

All rights reserved. No part of this book may be reproduced, scanned or distributed in any form, including digital and electronic or mechanical, including photocopying, recording, or by any information storage and retrieval system, without the prior written consent of the Publisher, except for brief quotes for use in reviews.

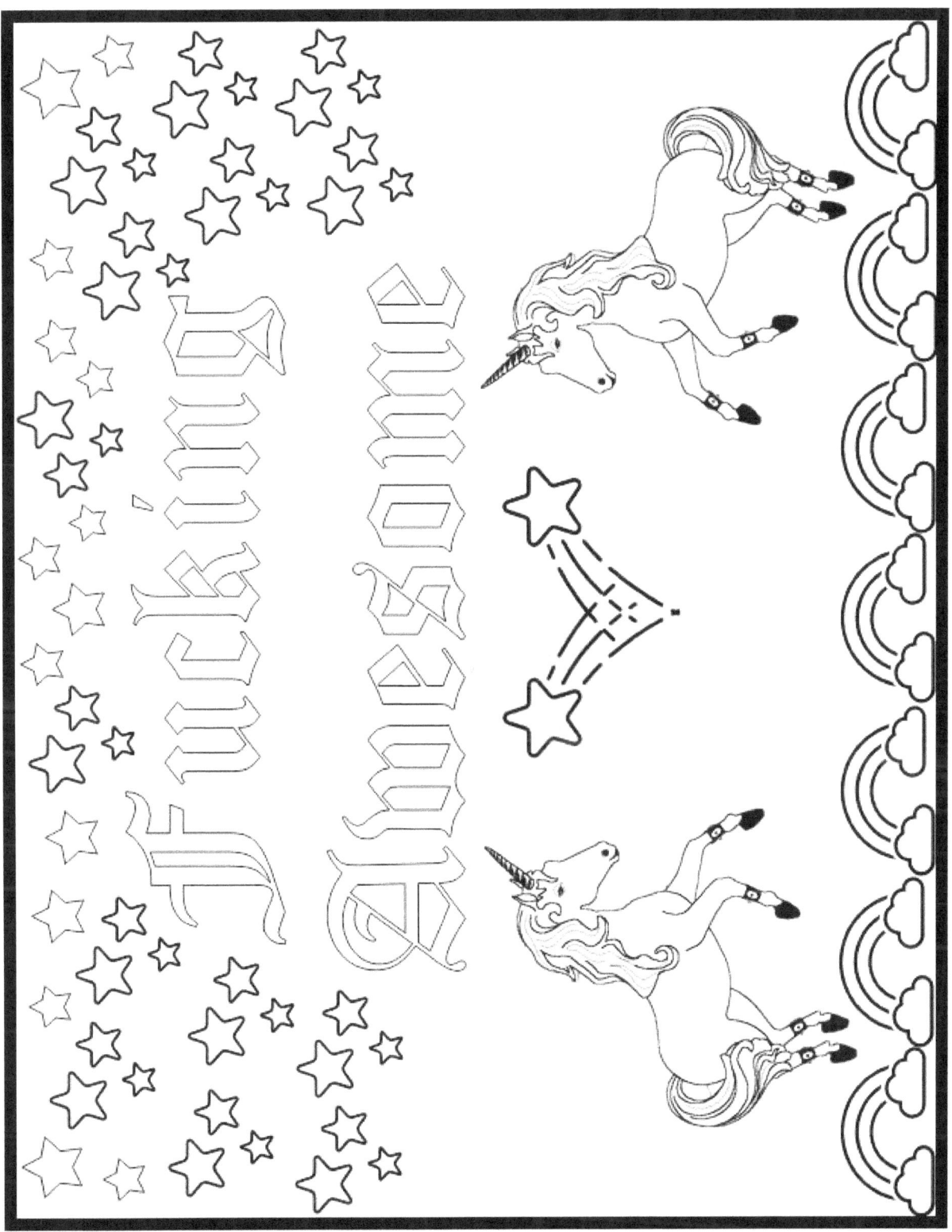

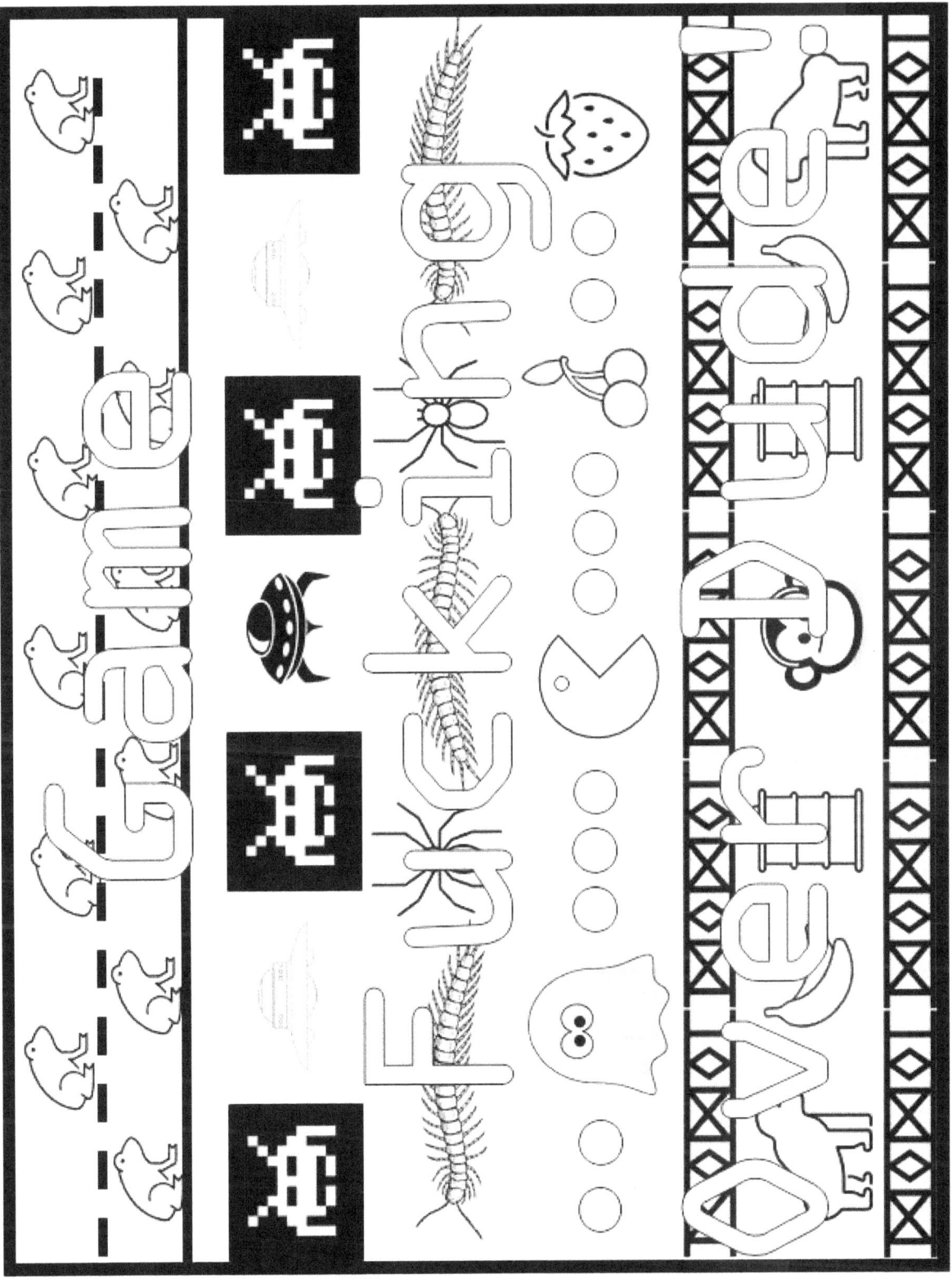

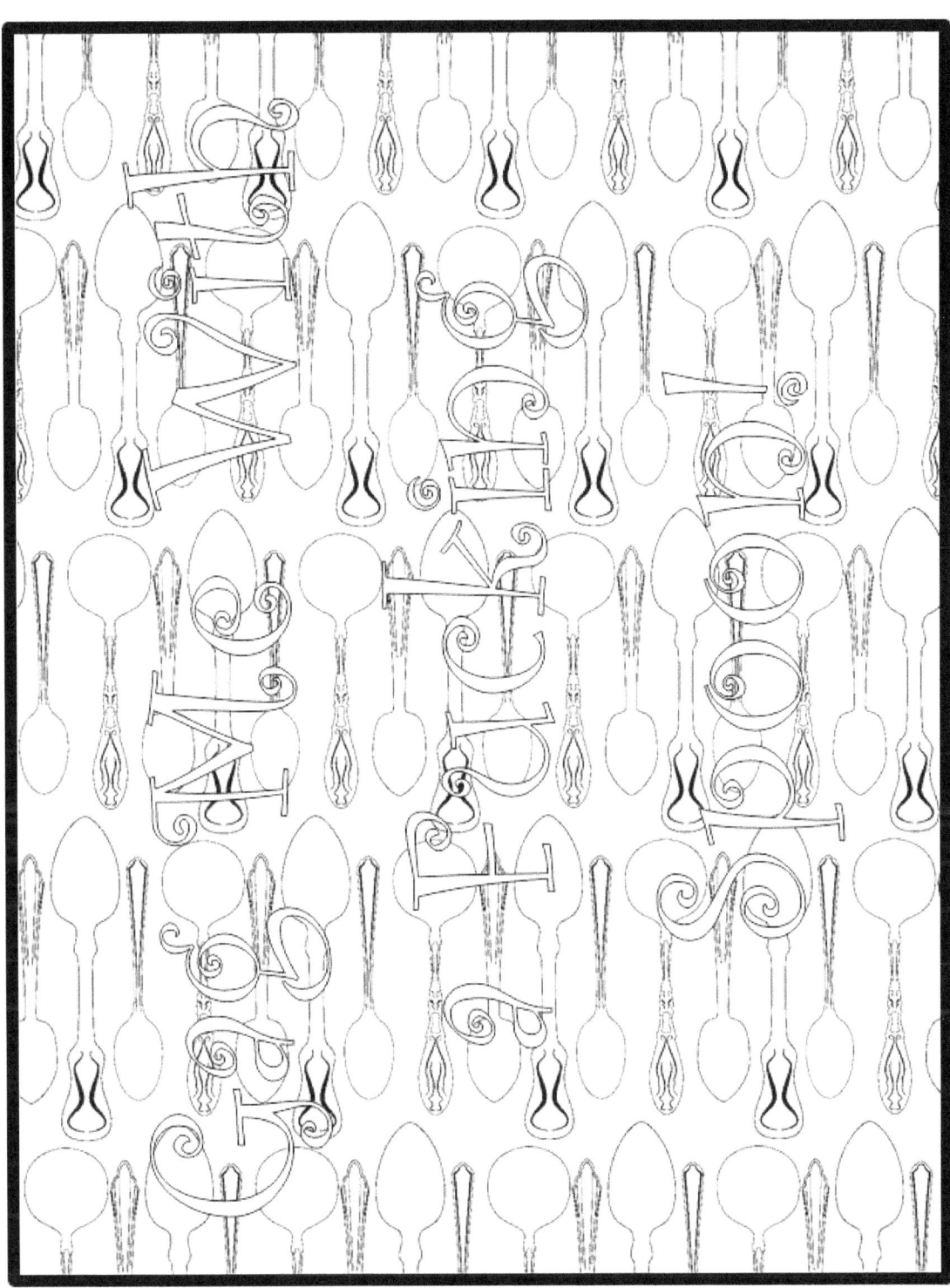

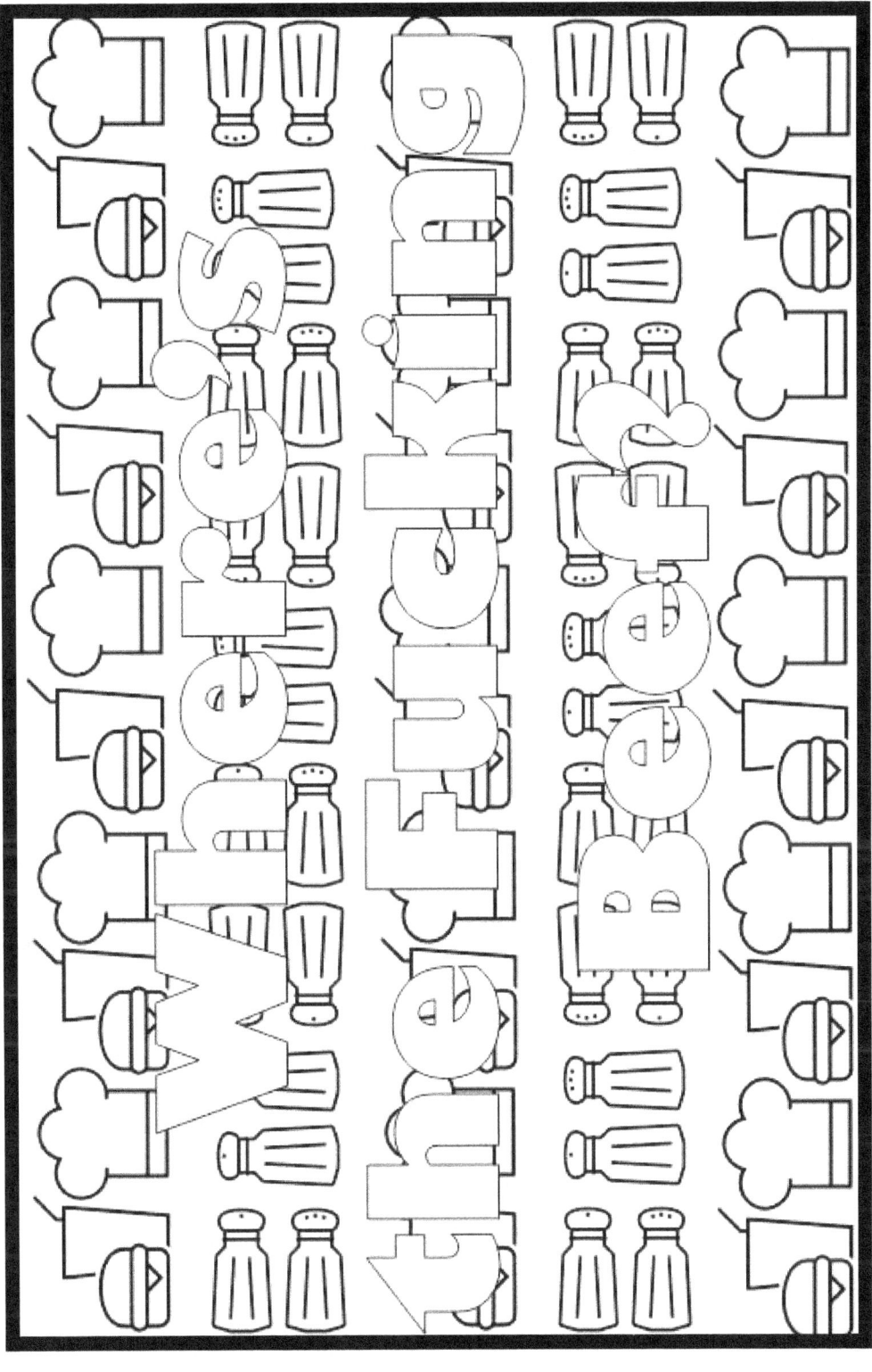

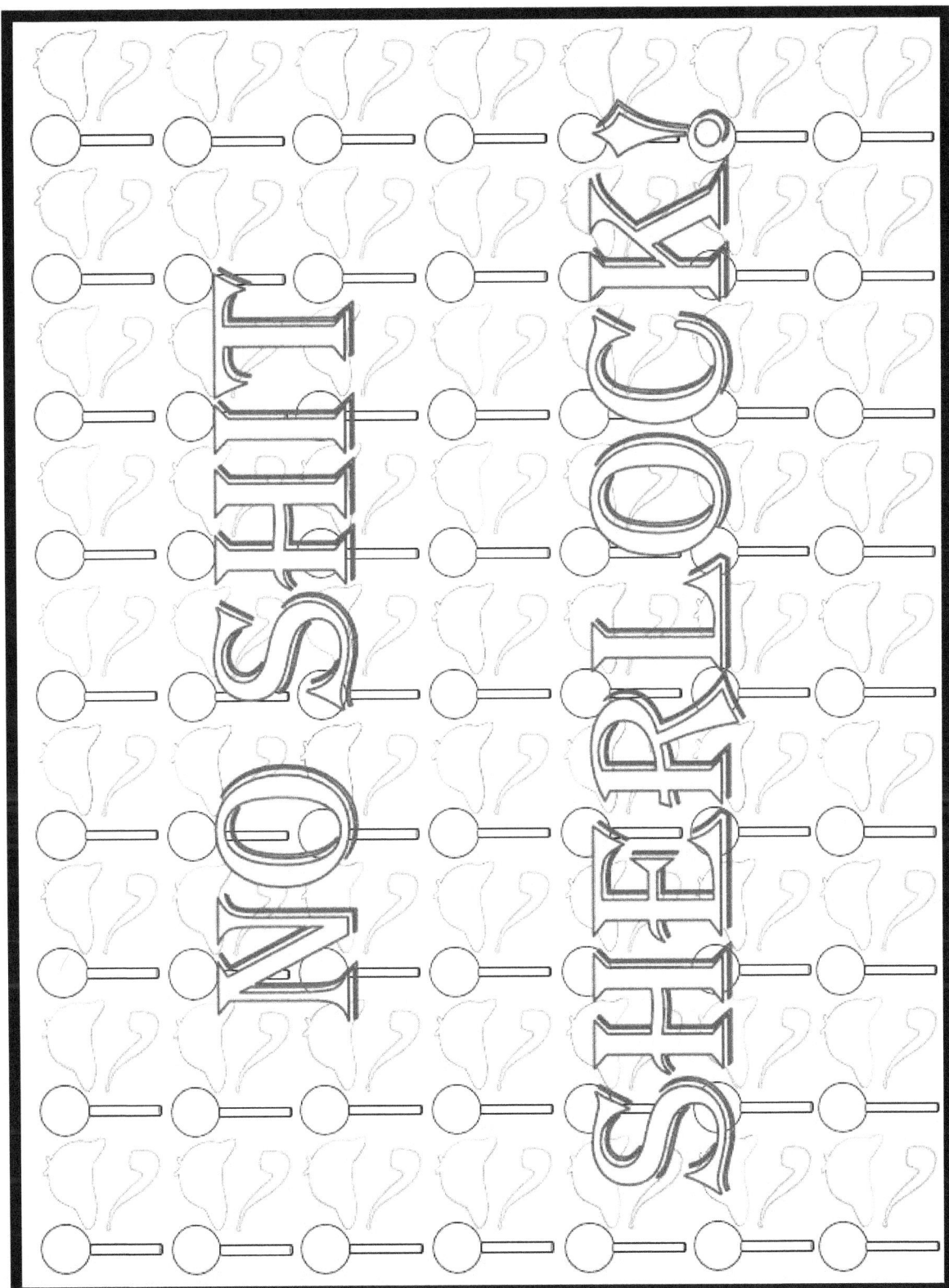

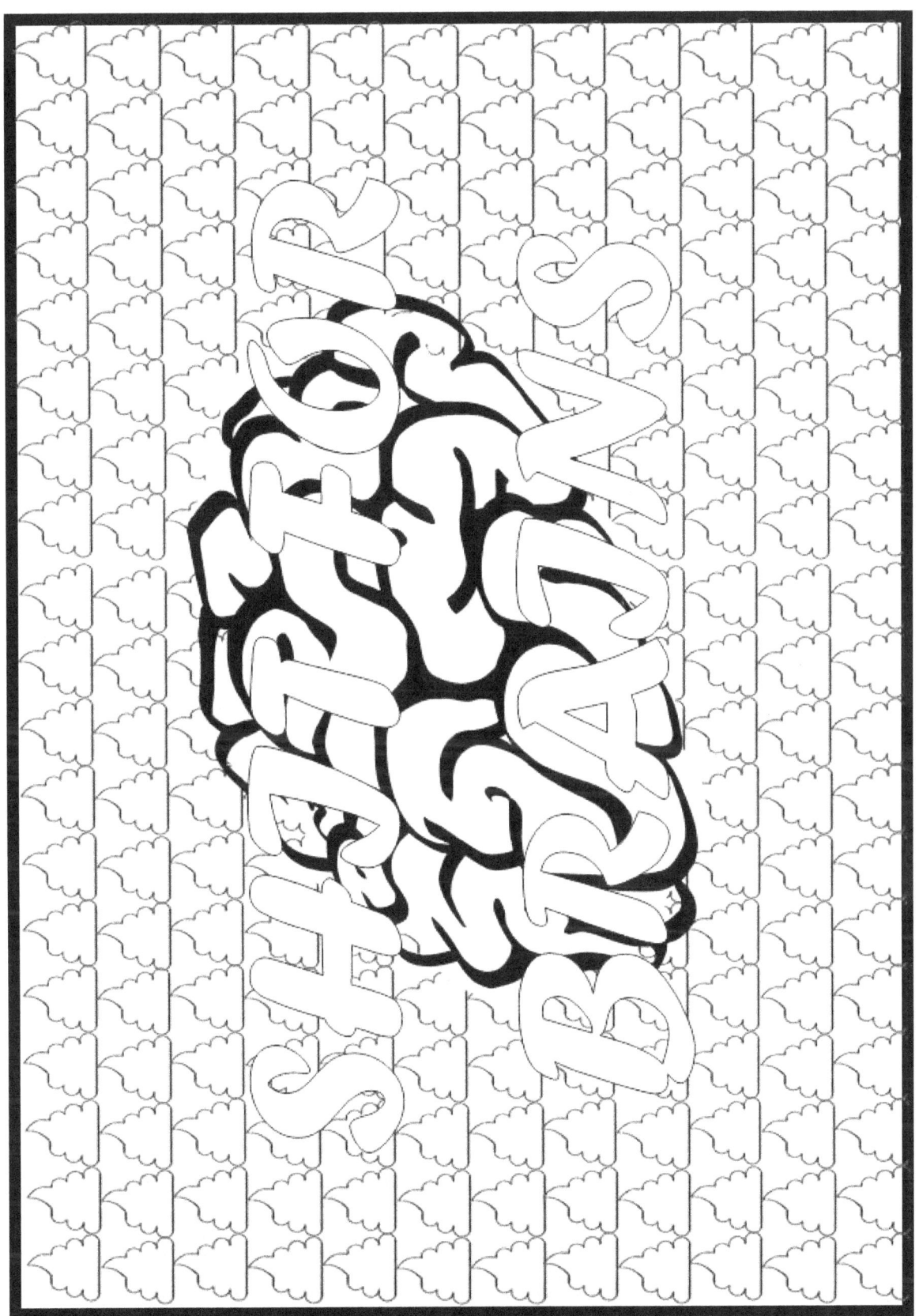

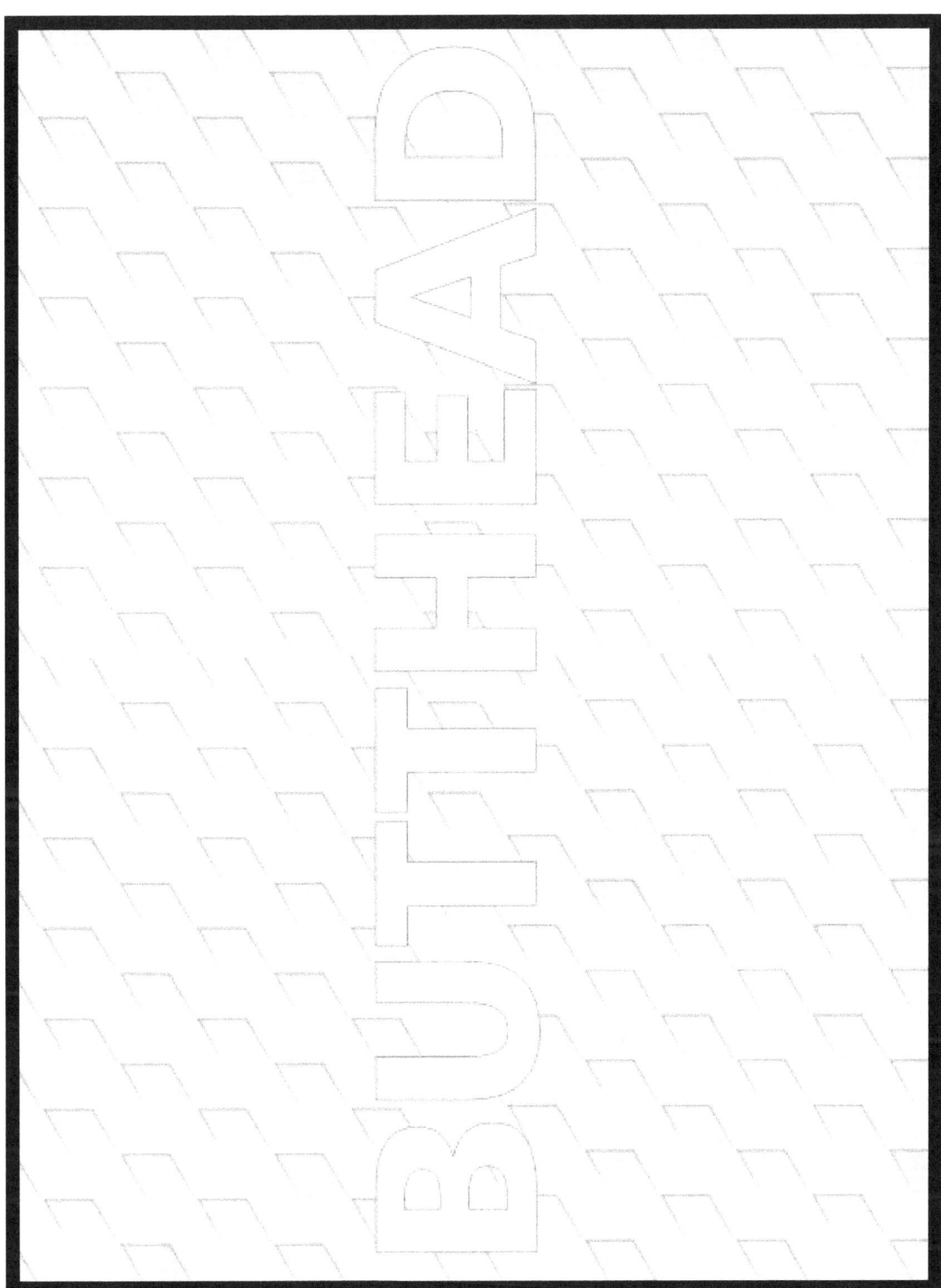

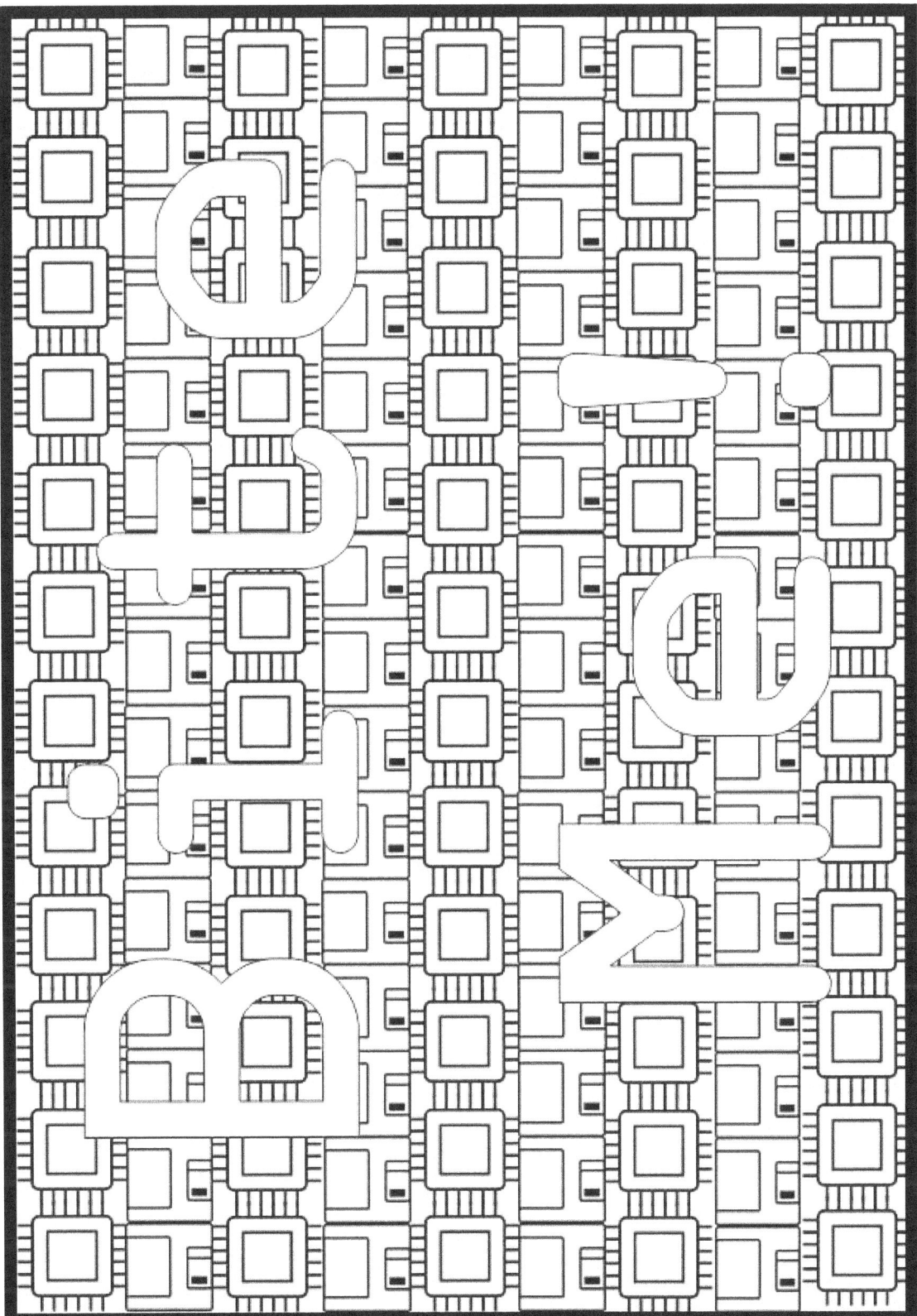

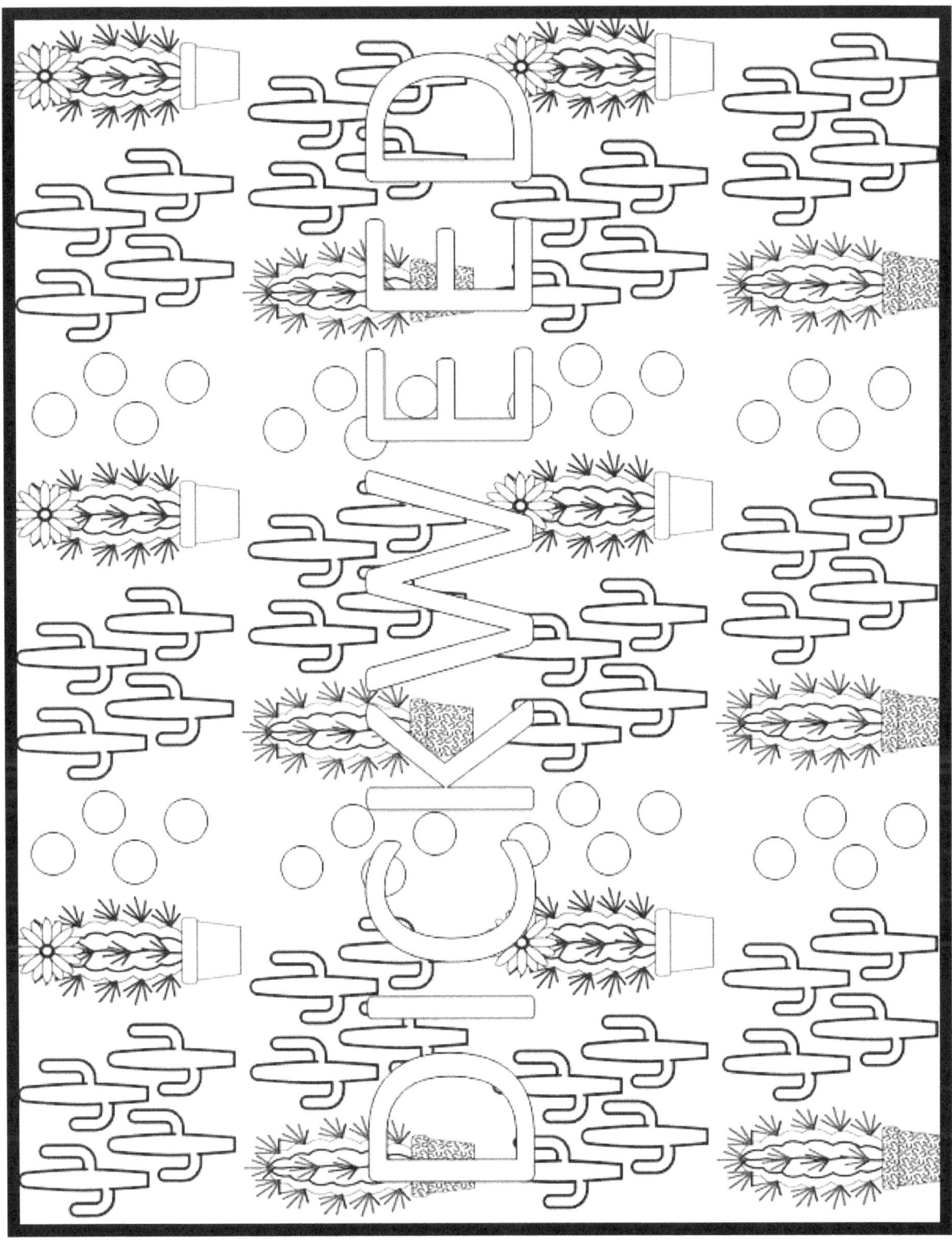

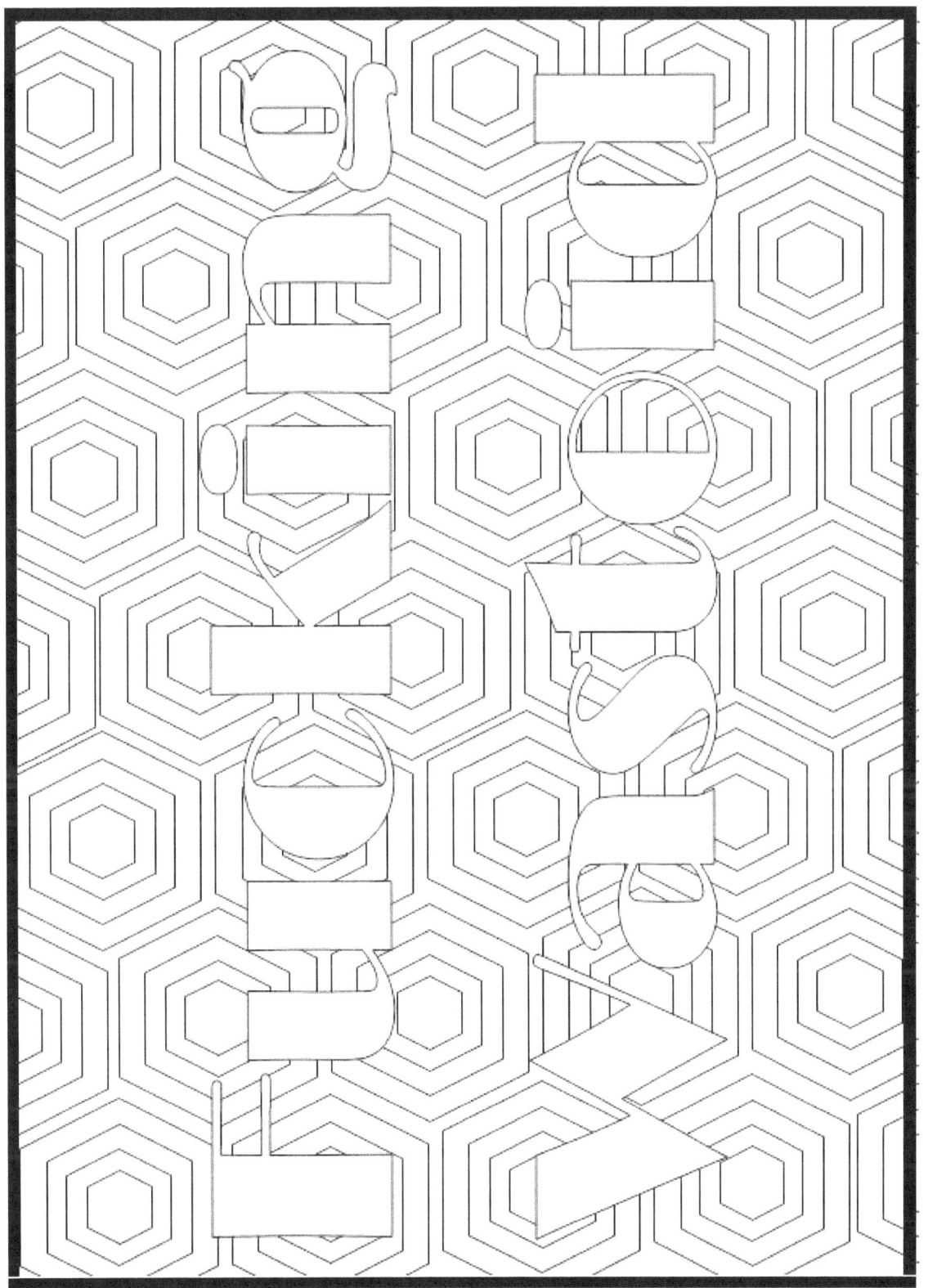

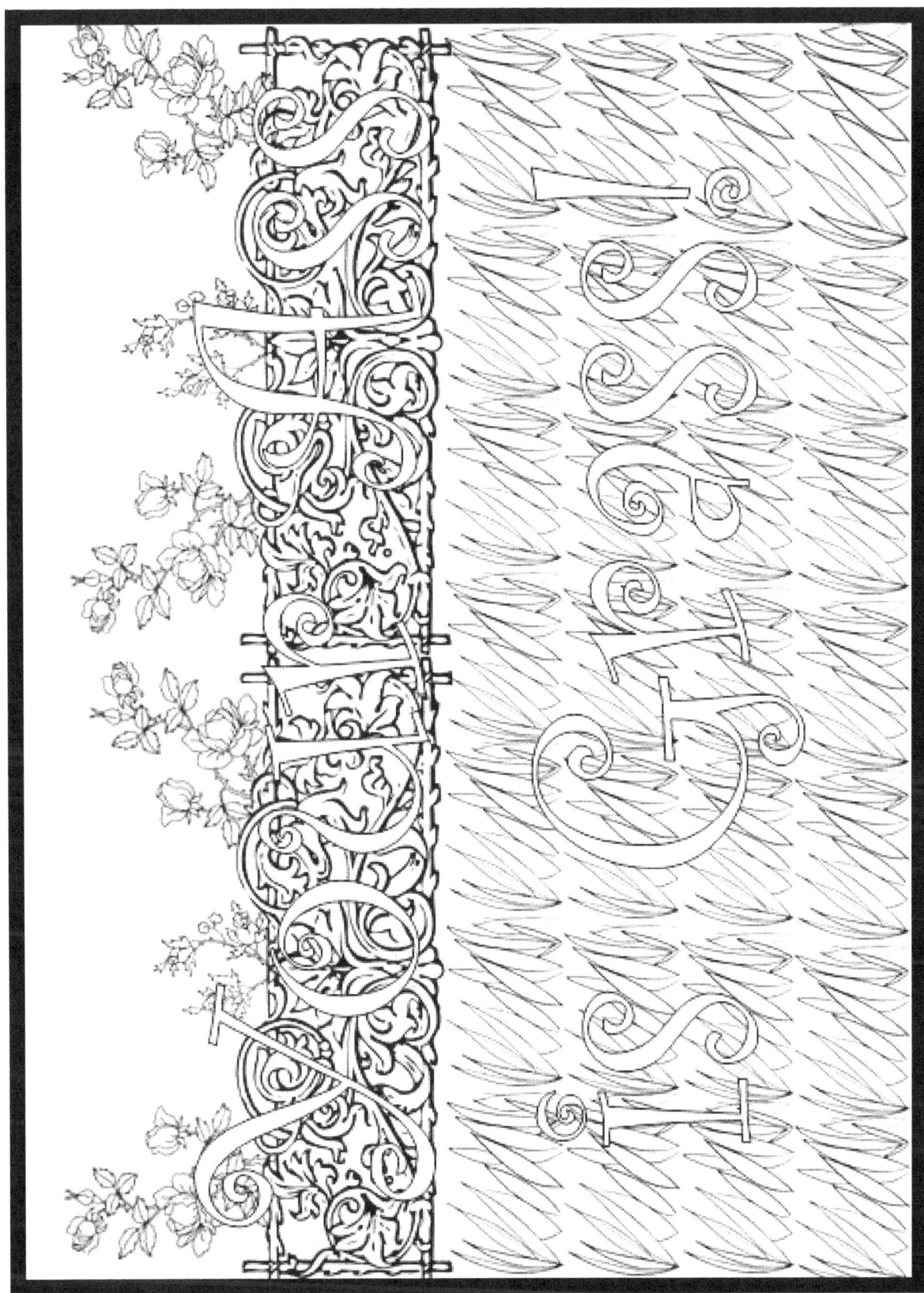

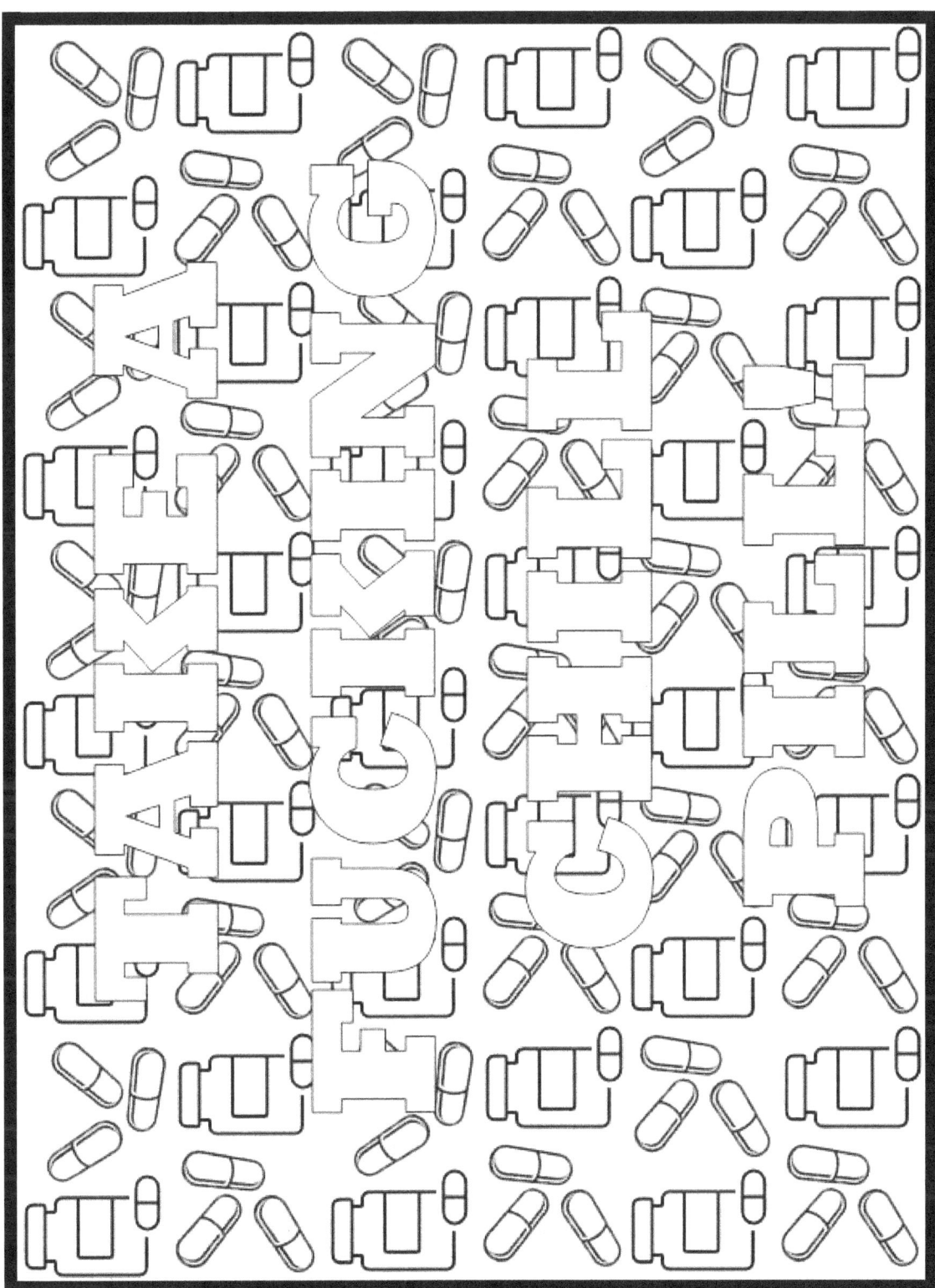

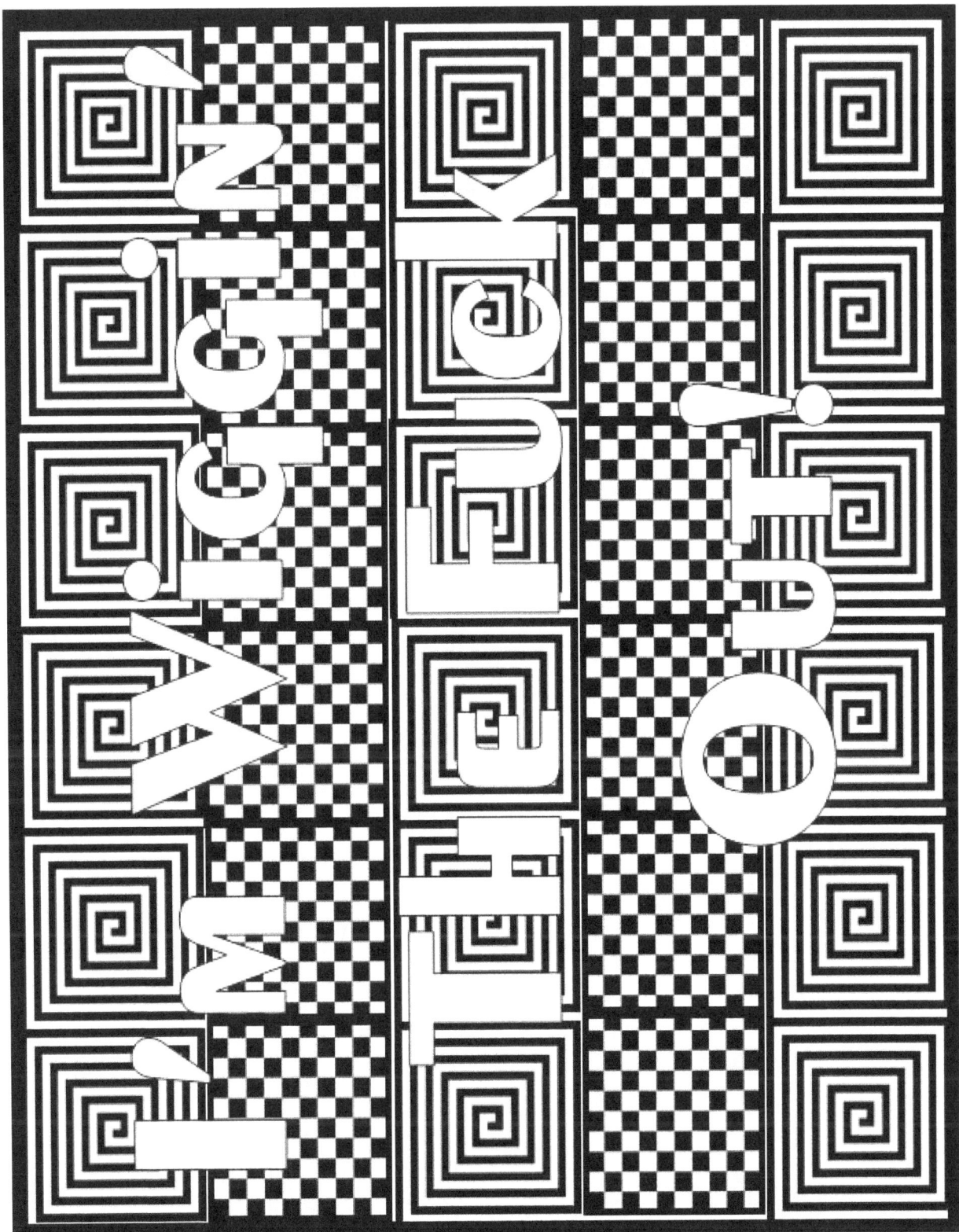

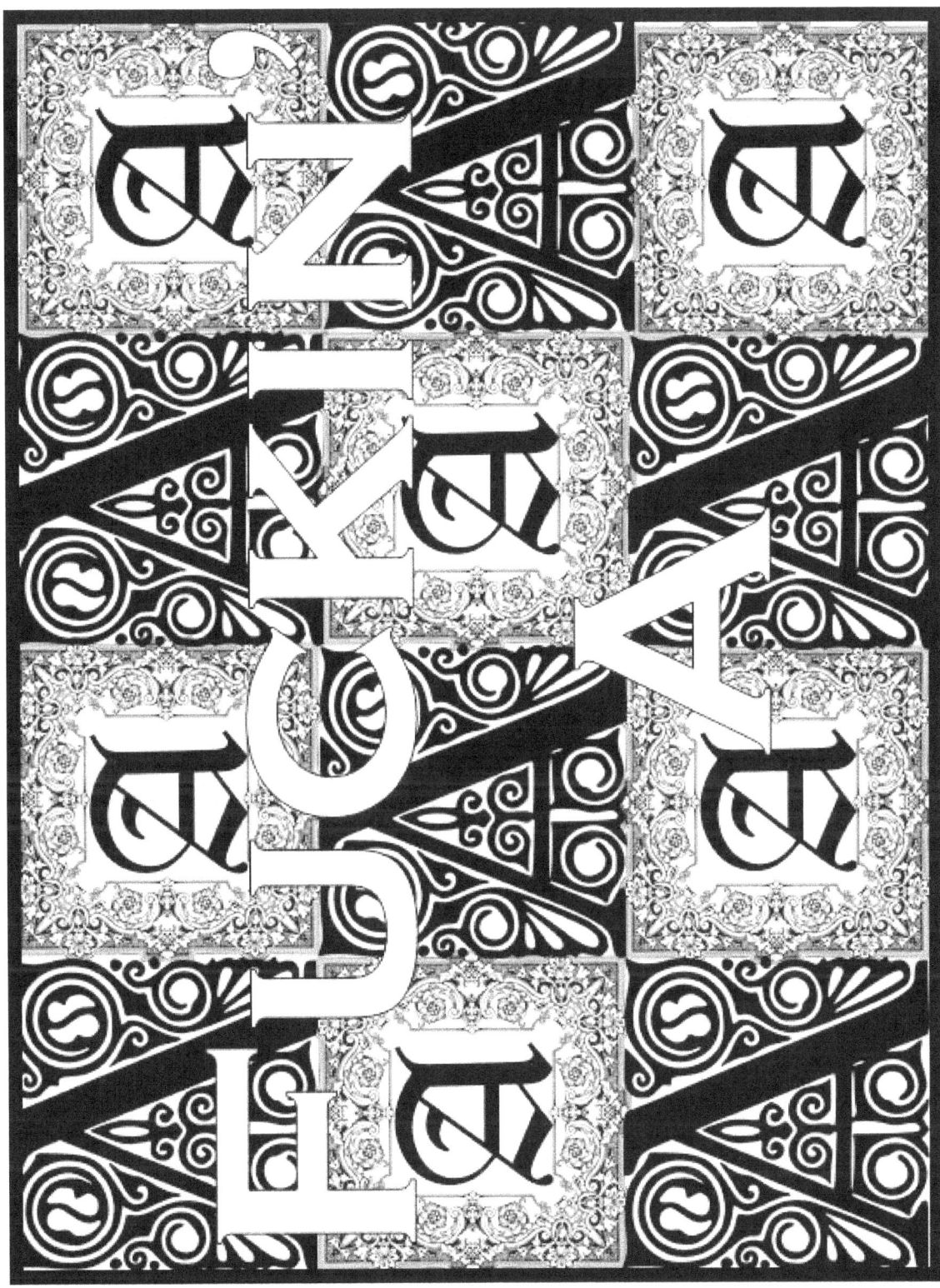

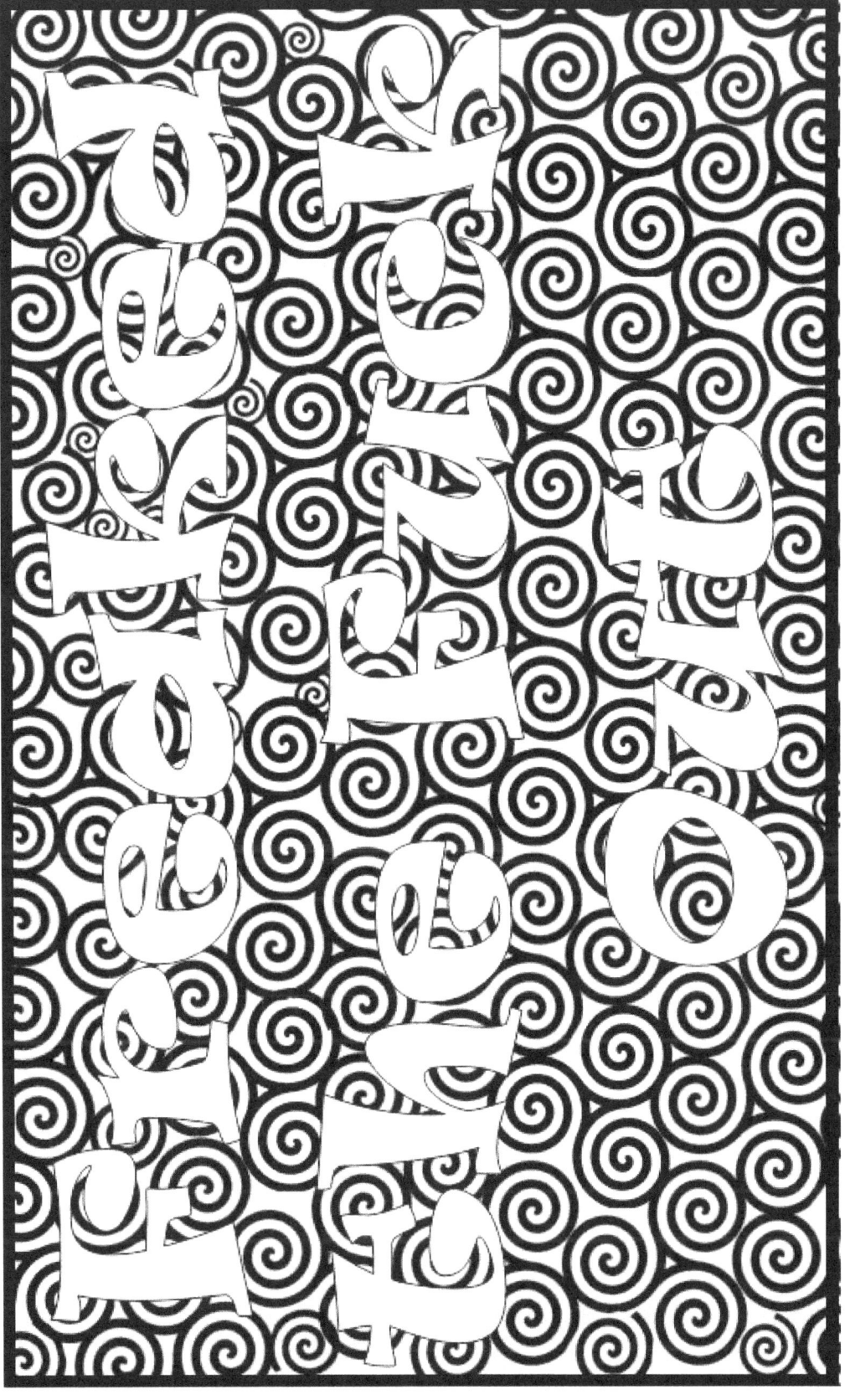

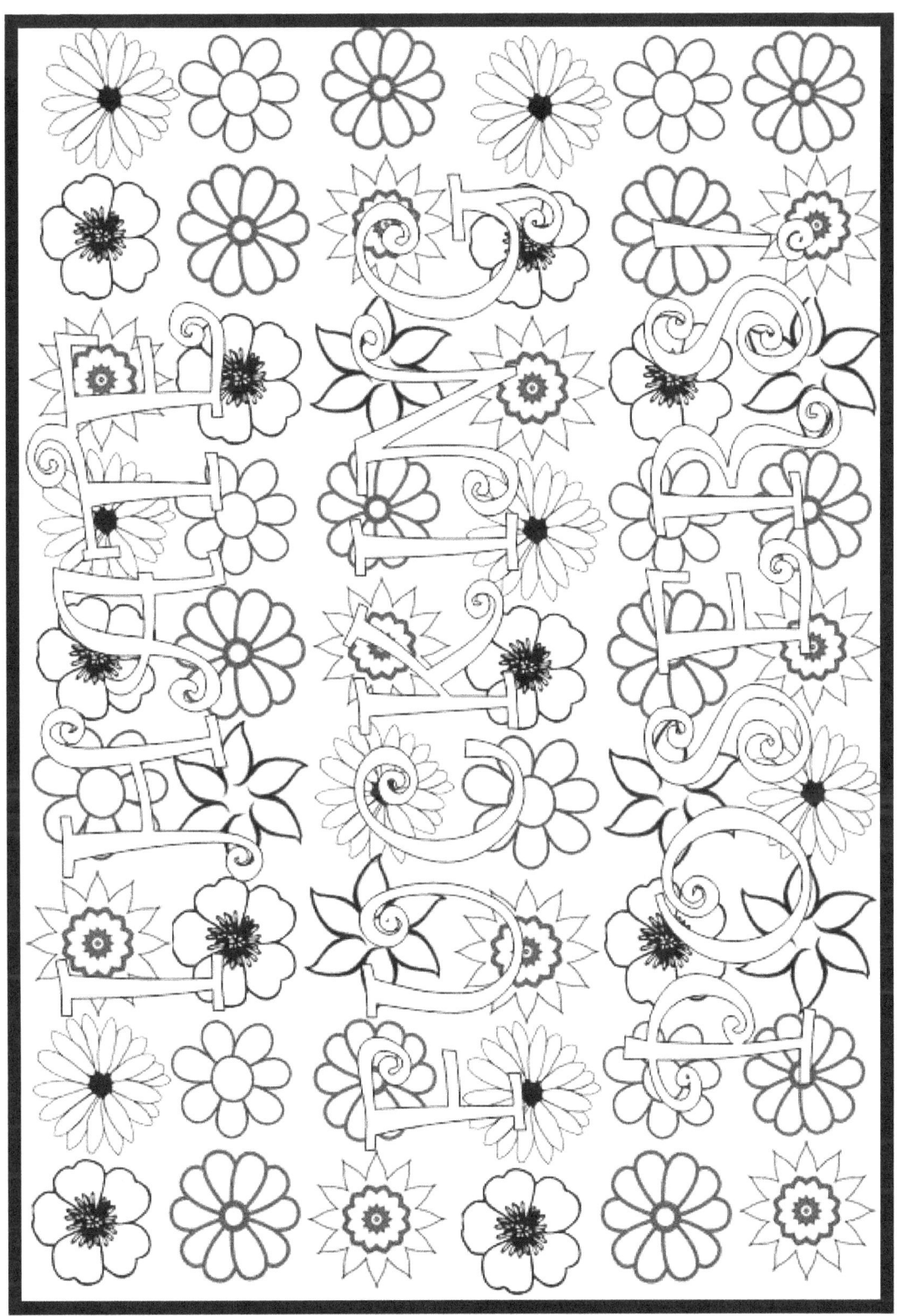

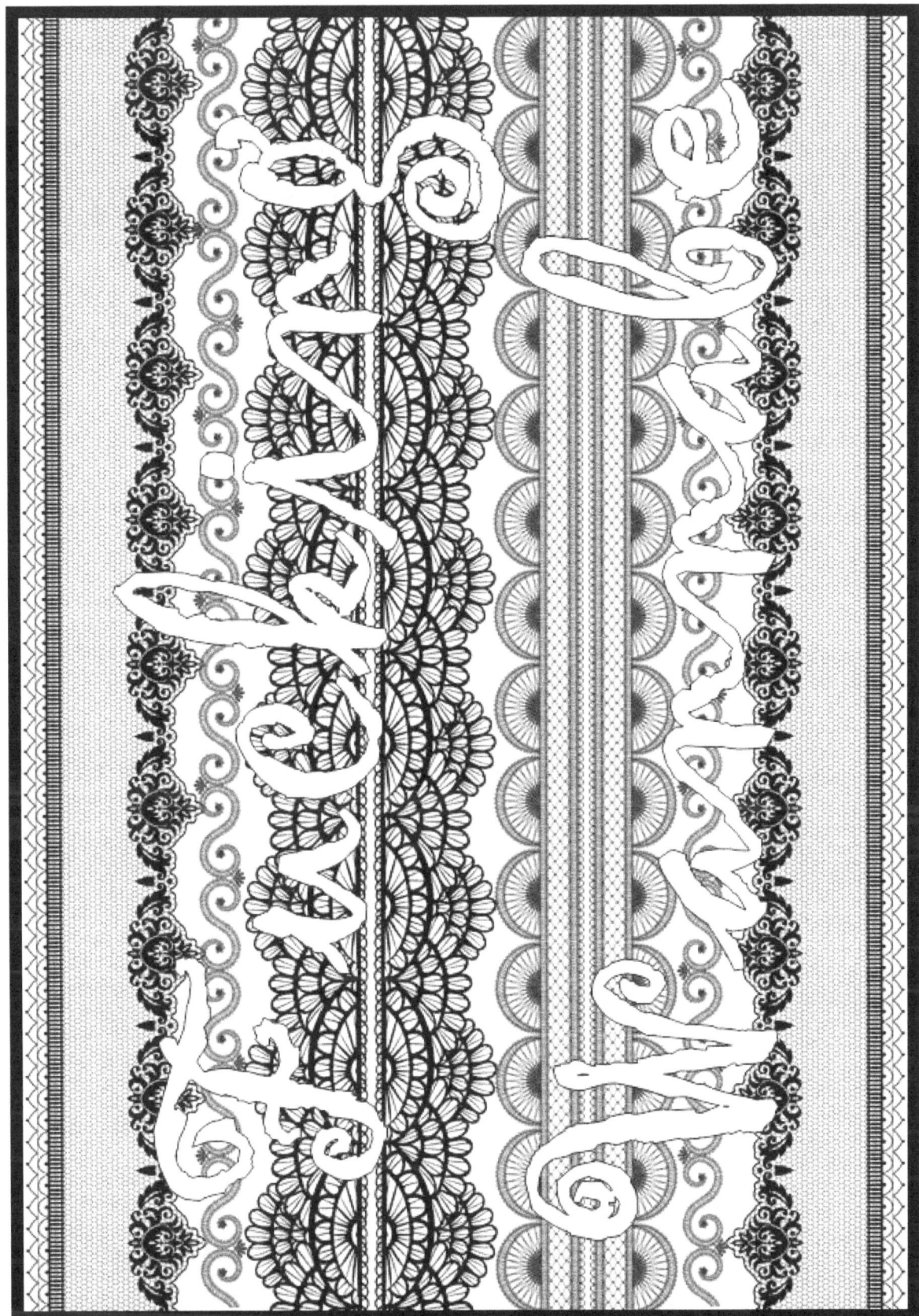

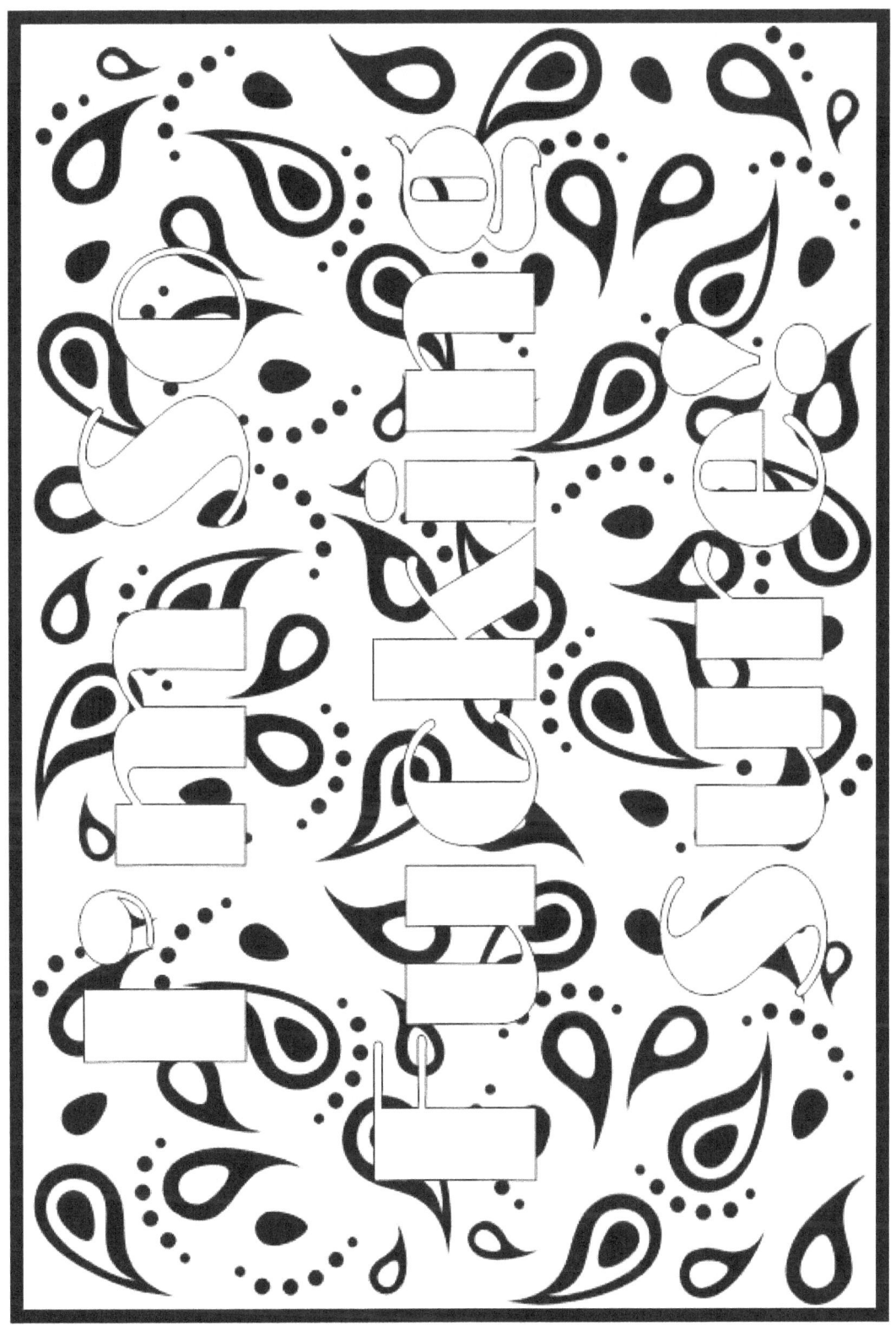

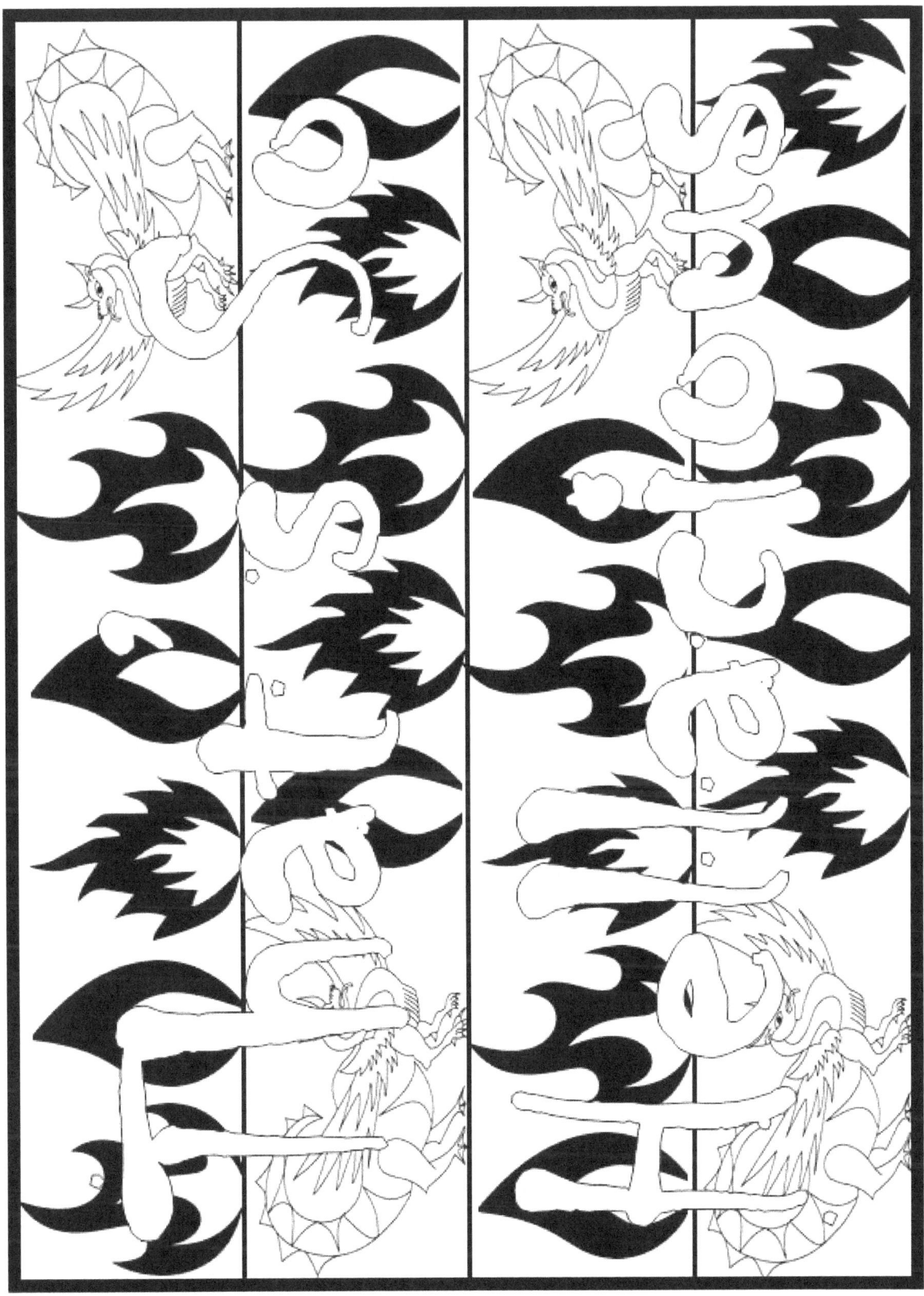

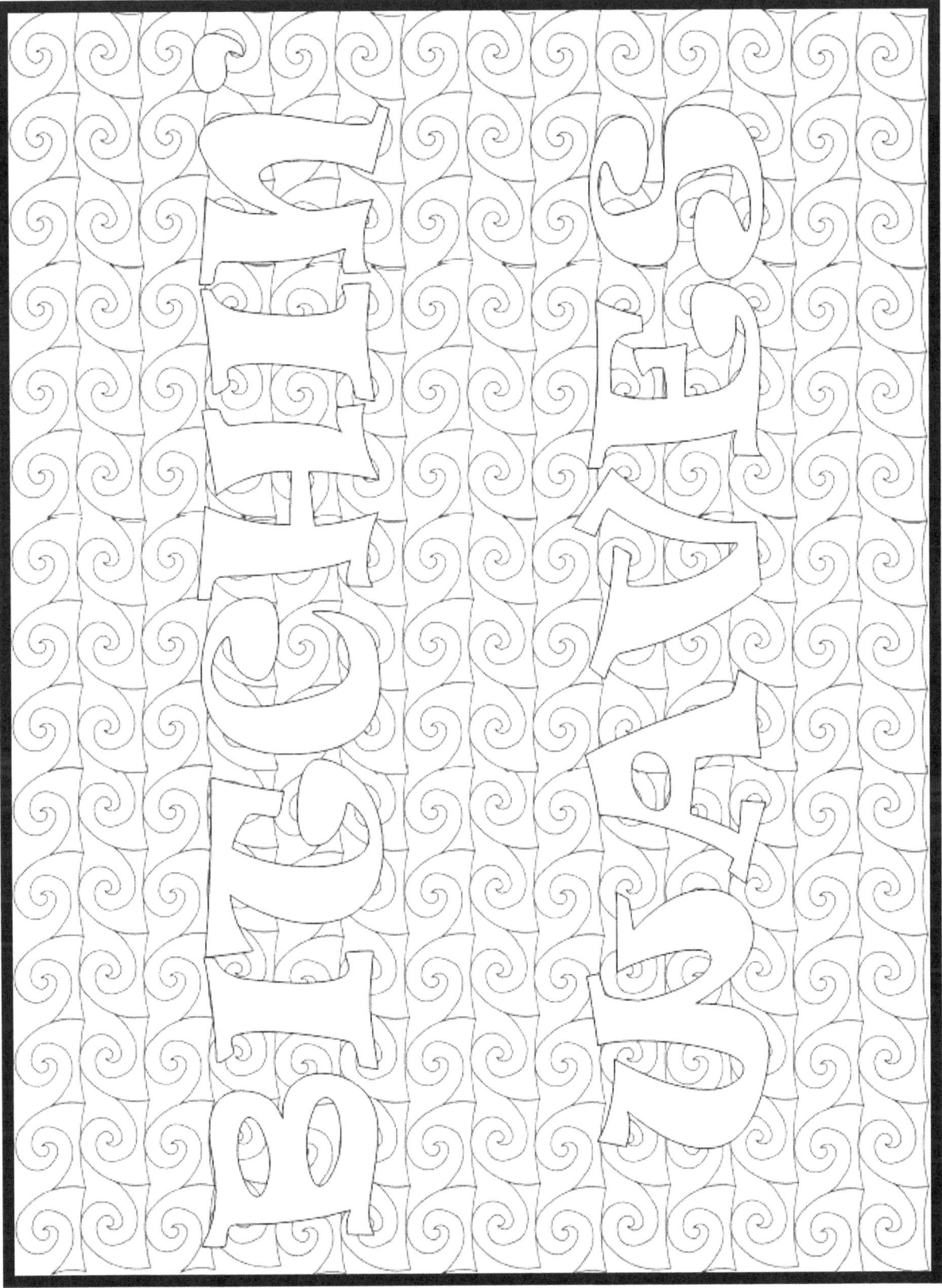

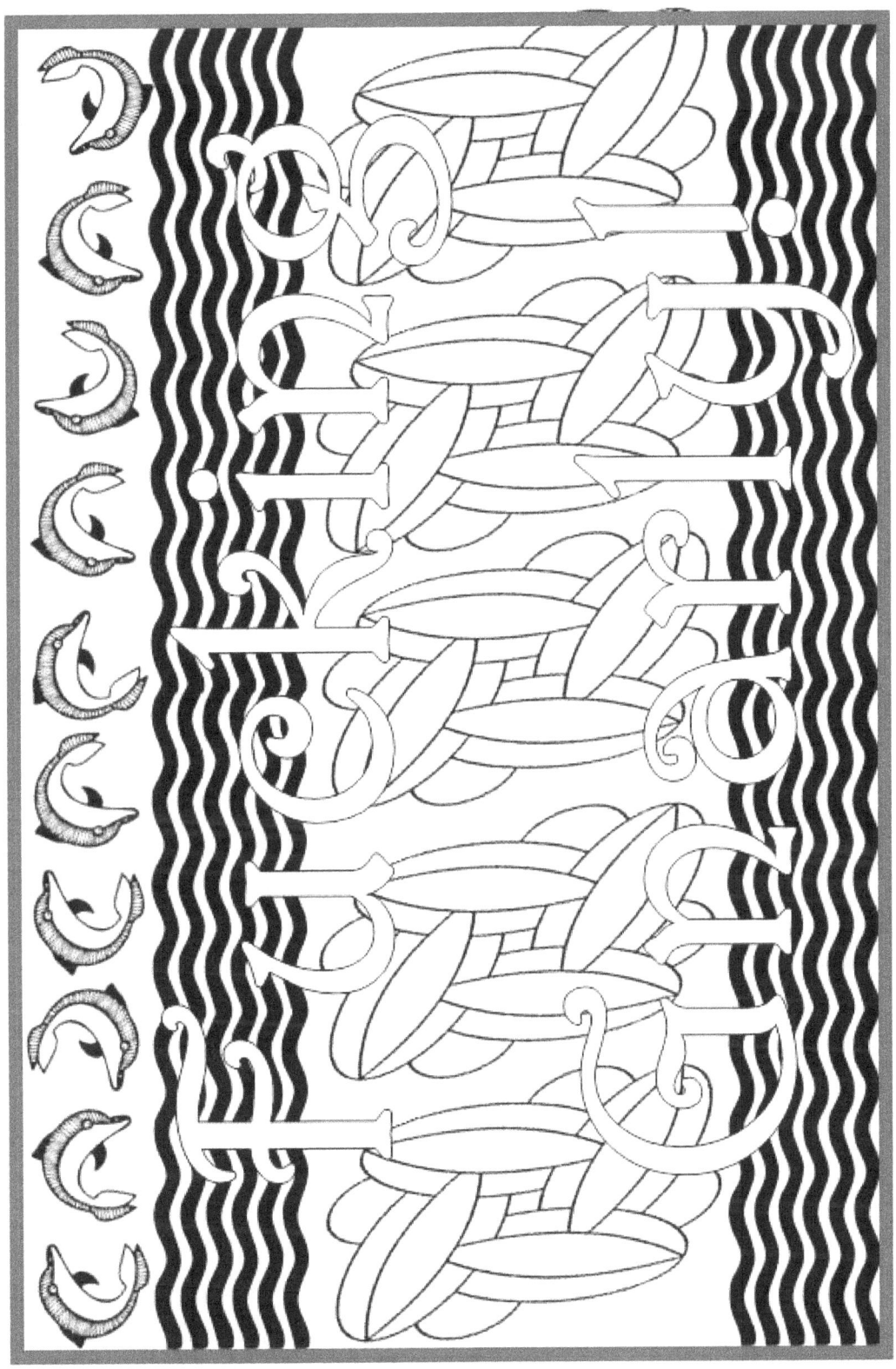

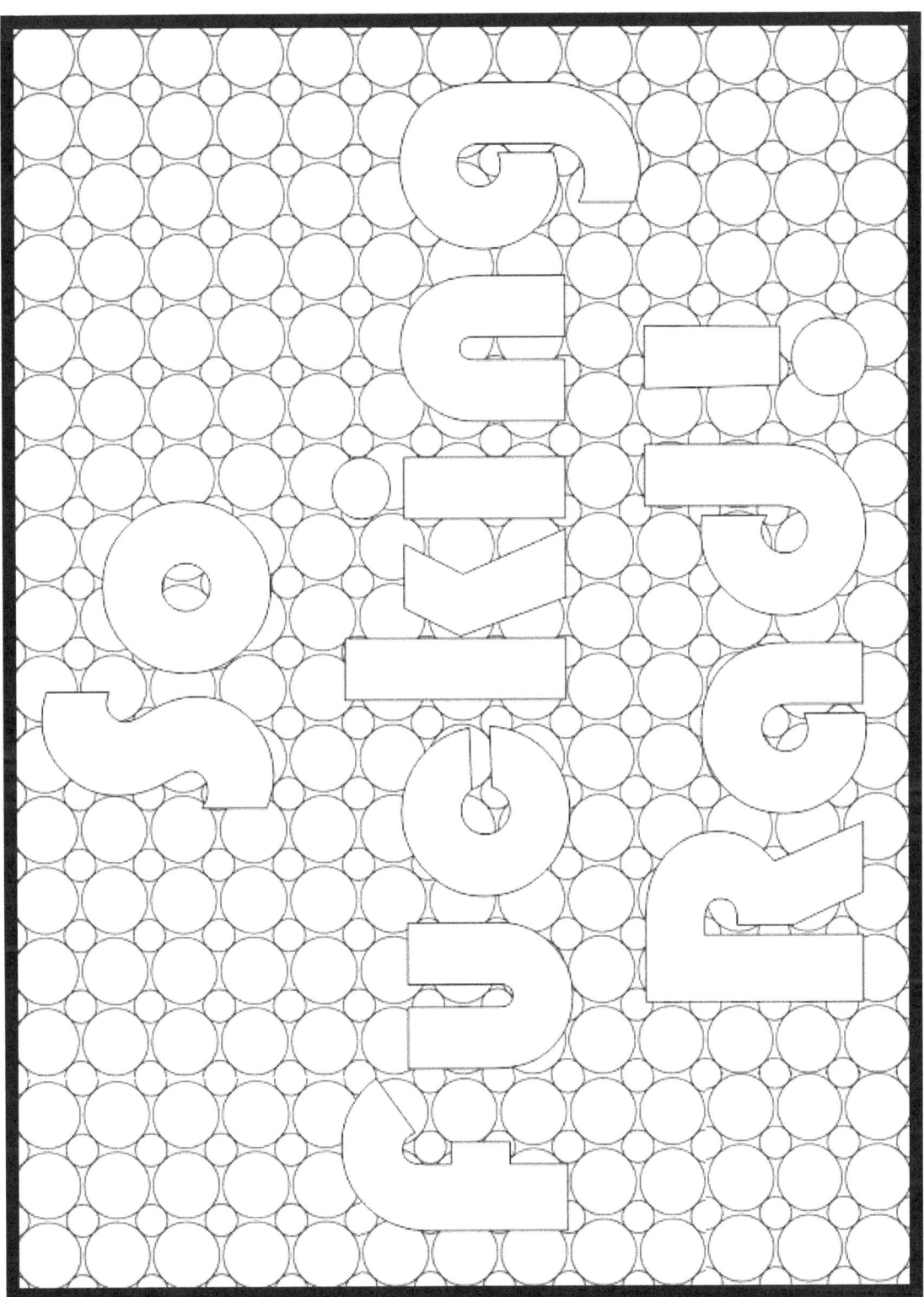

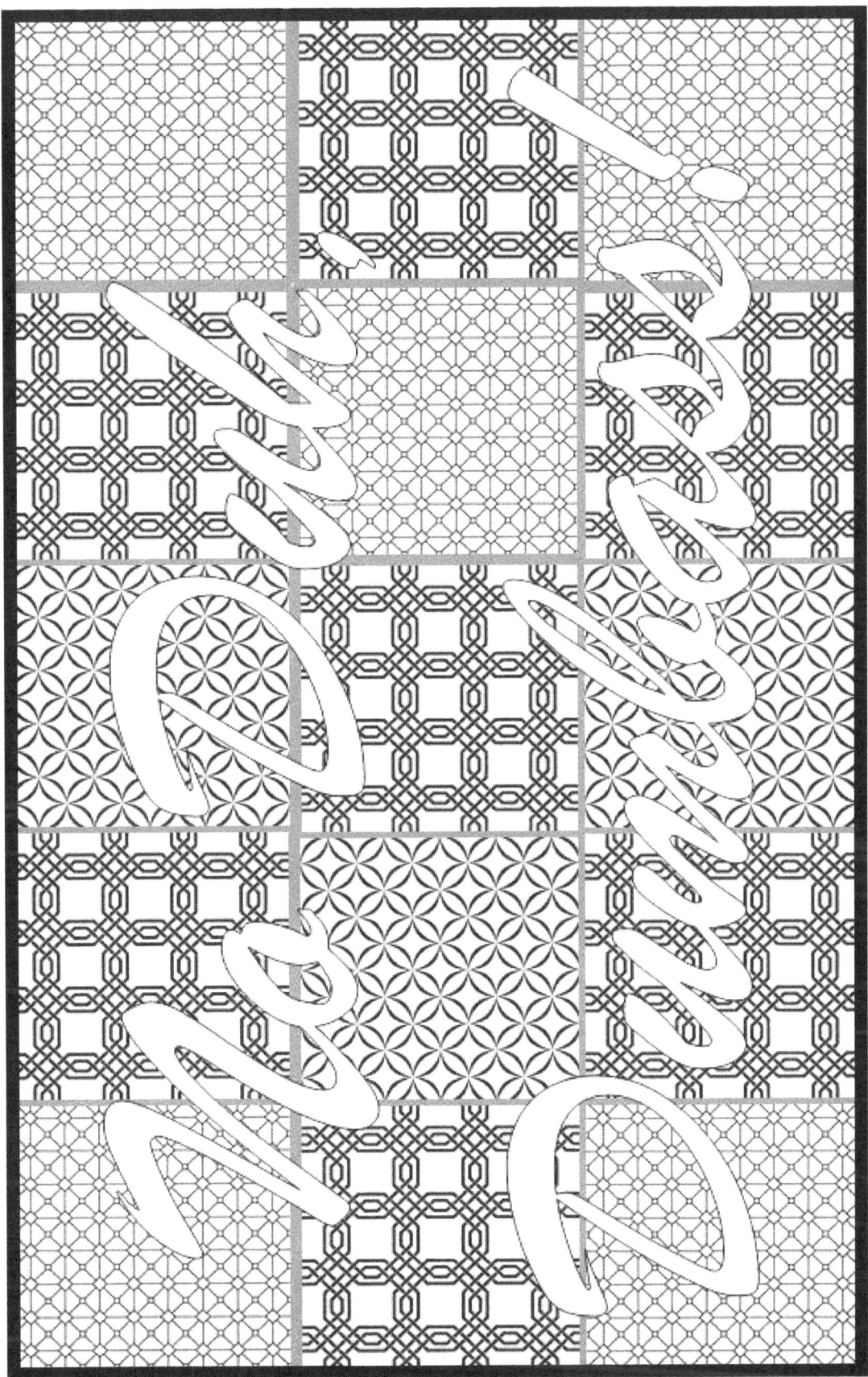

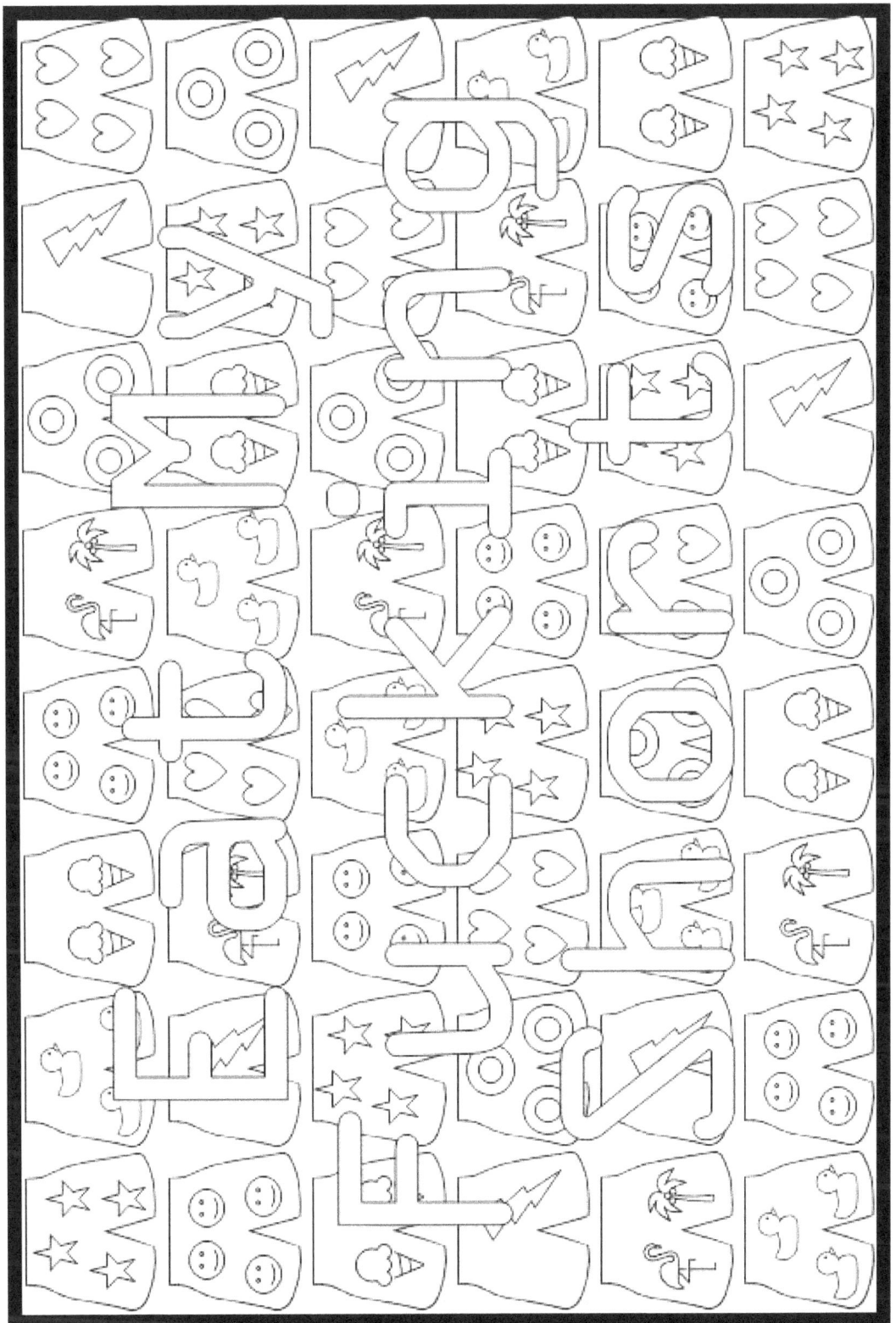

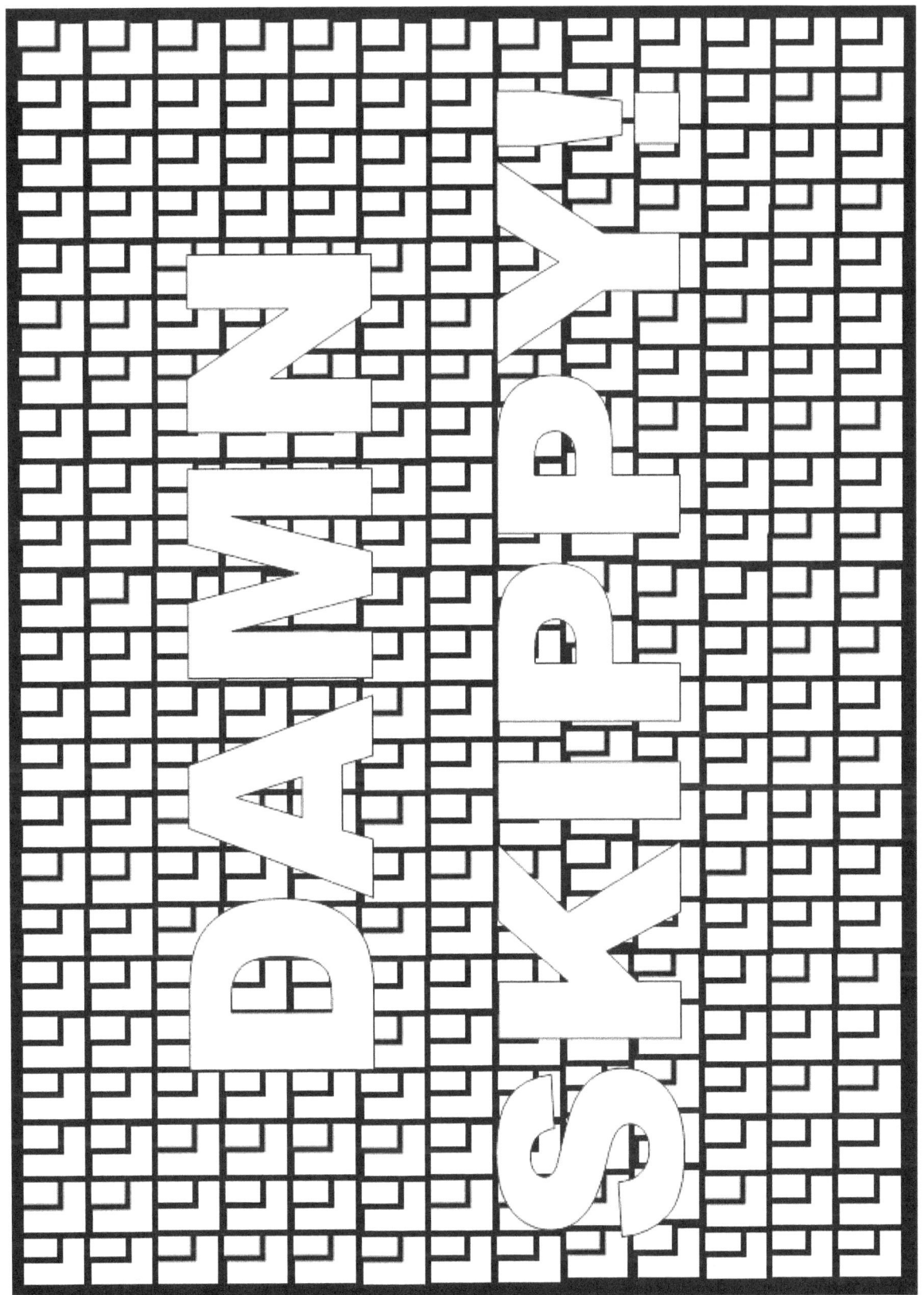

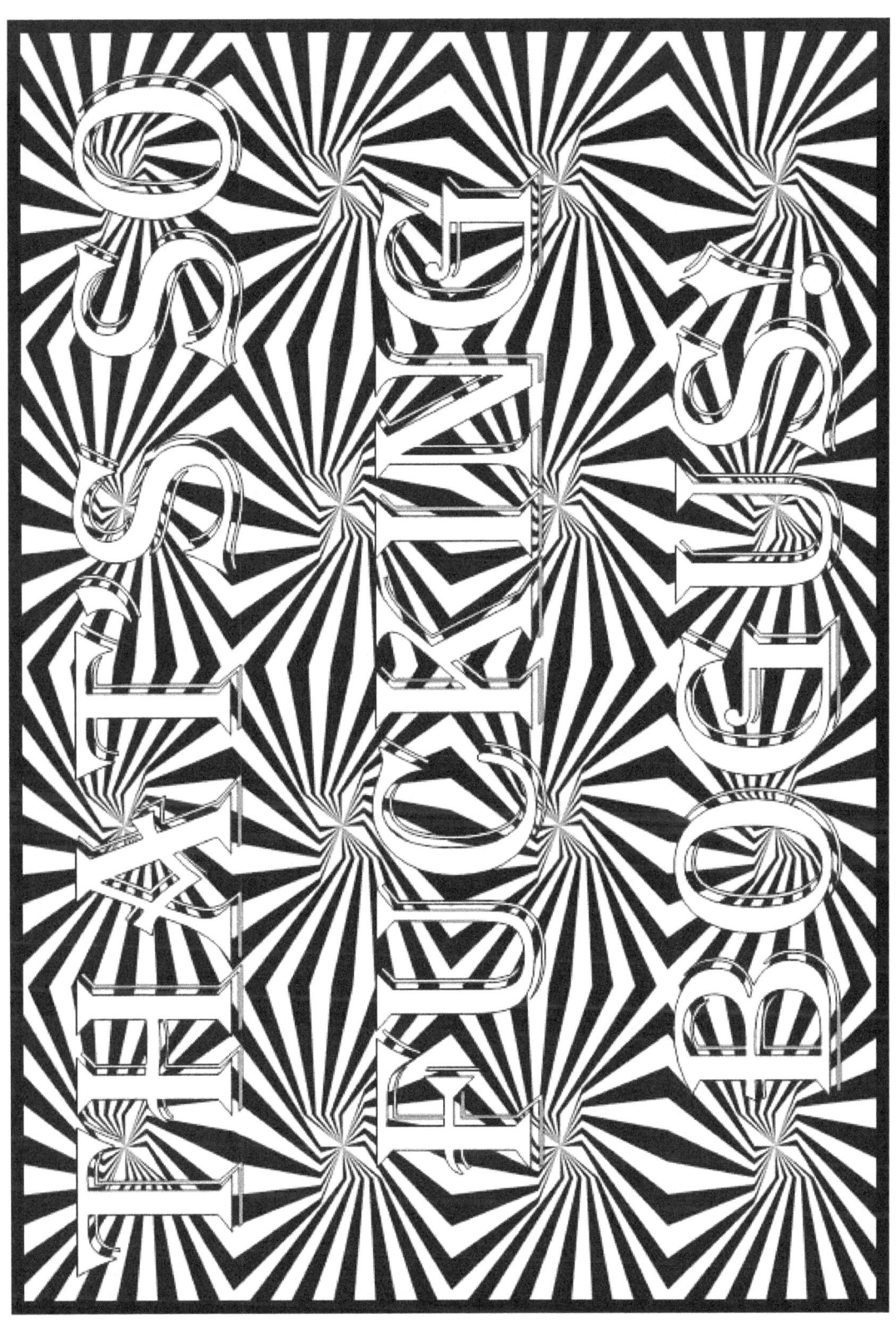

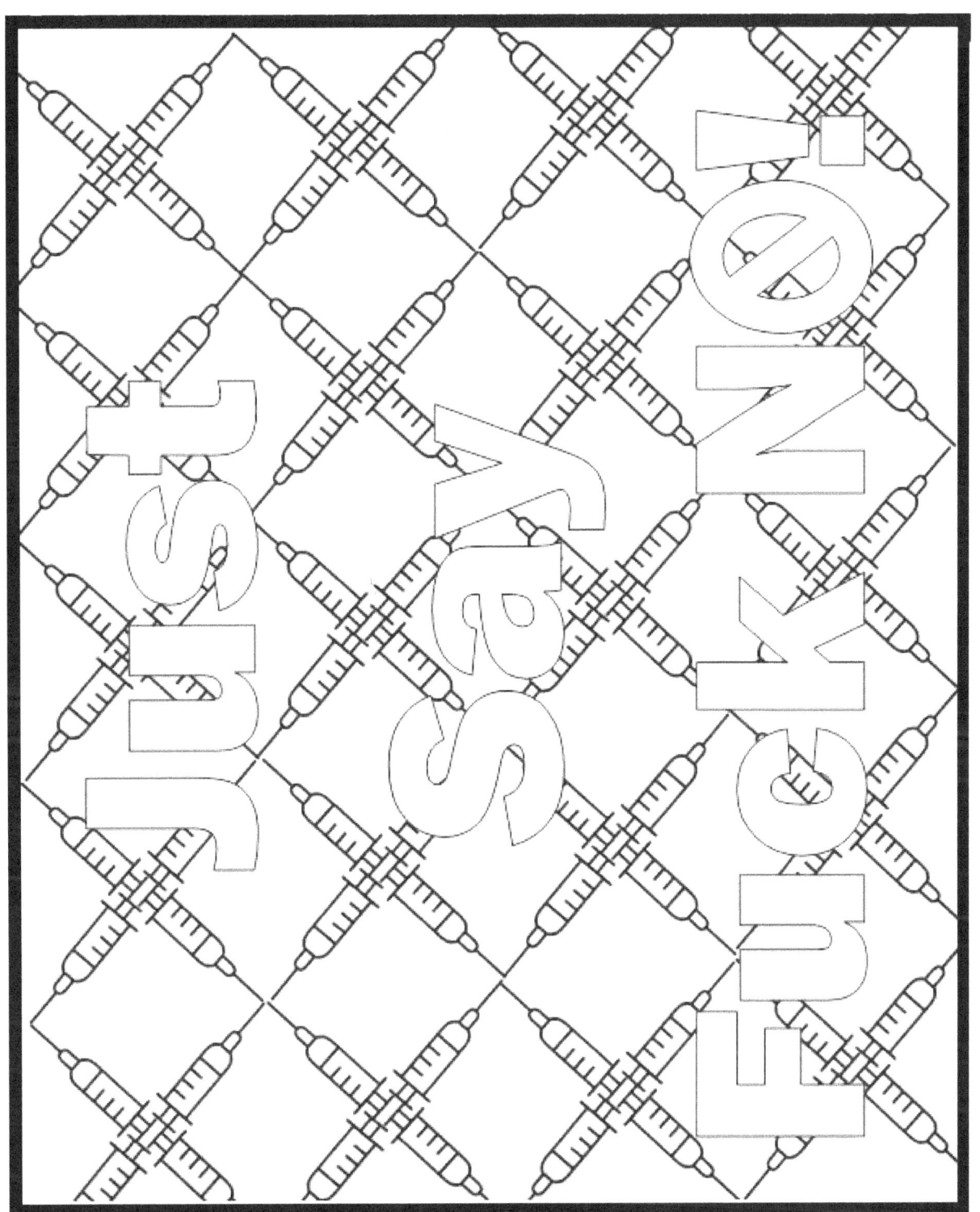

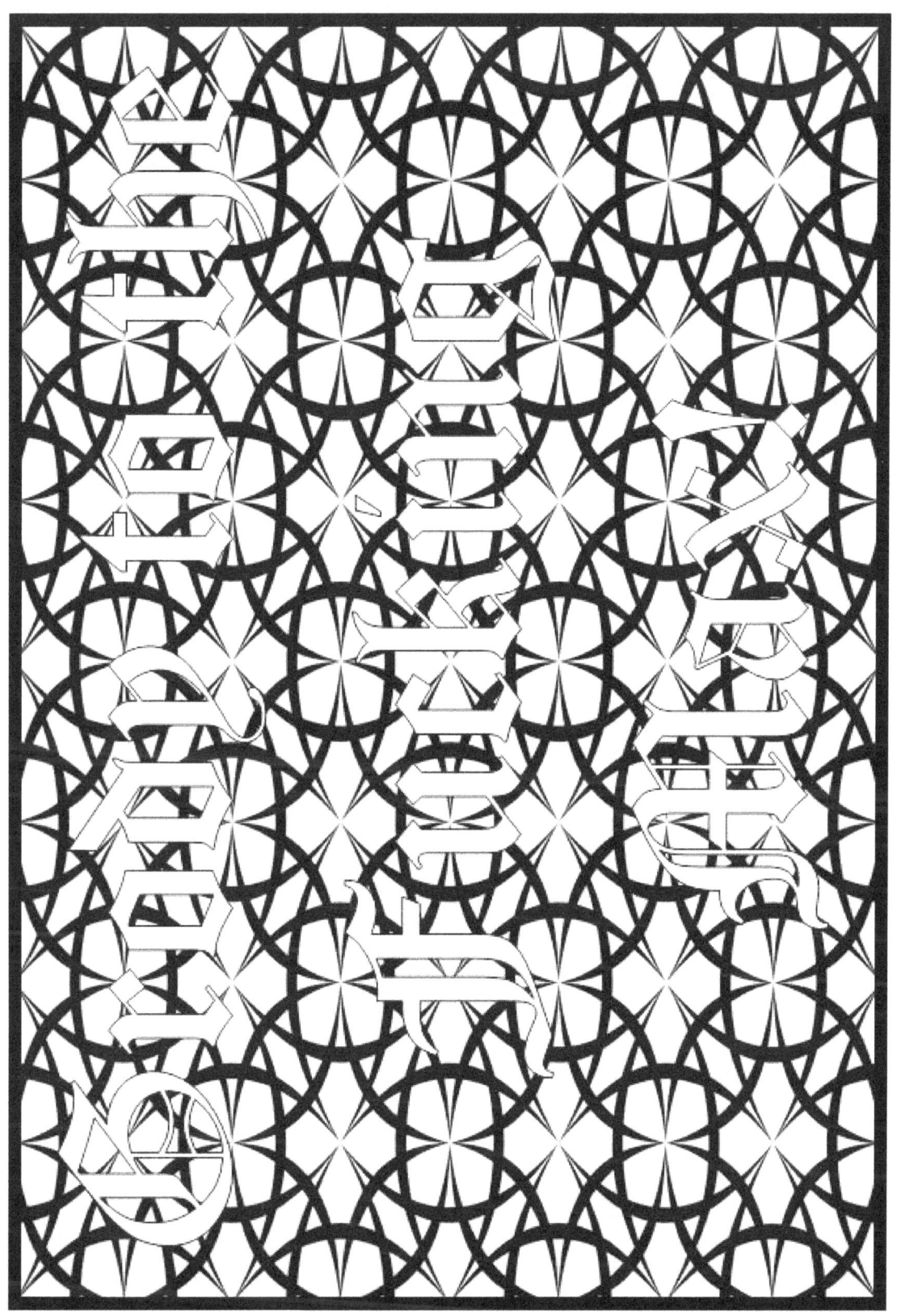

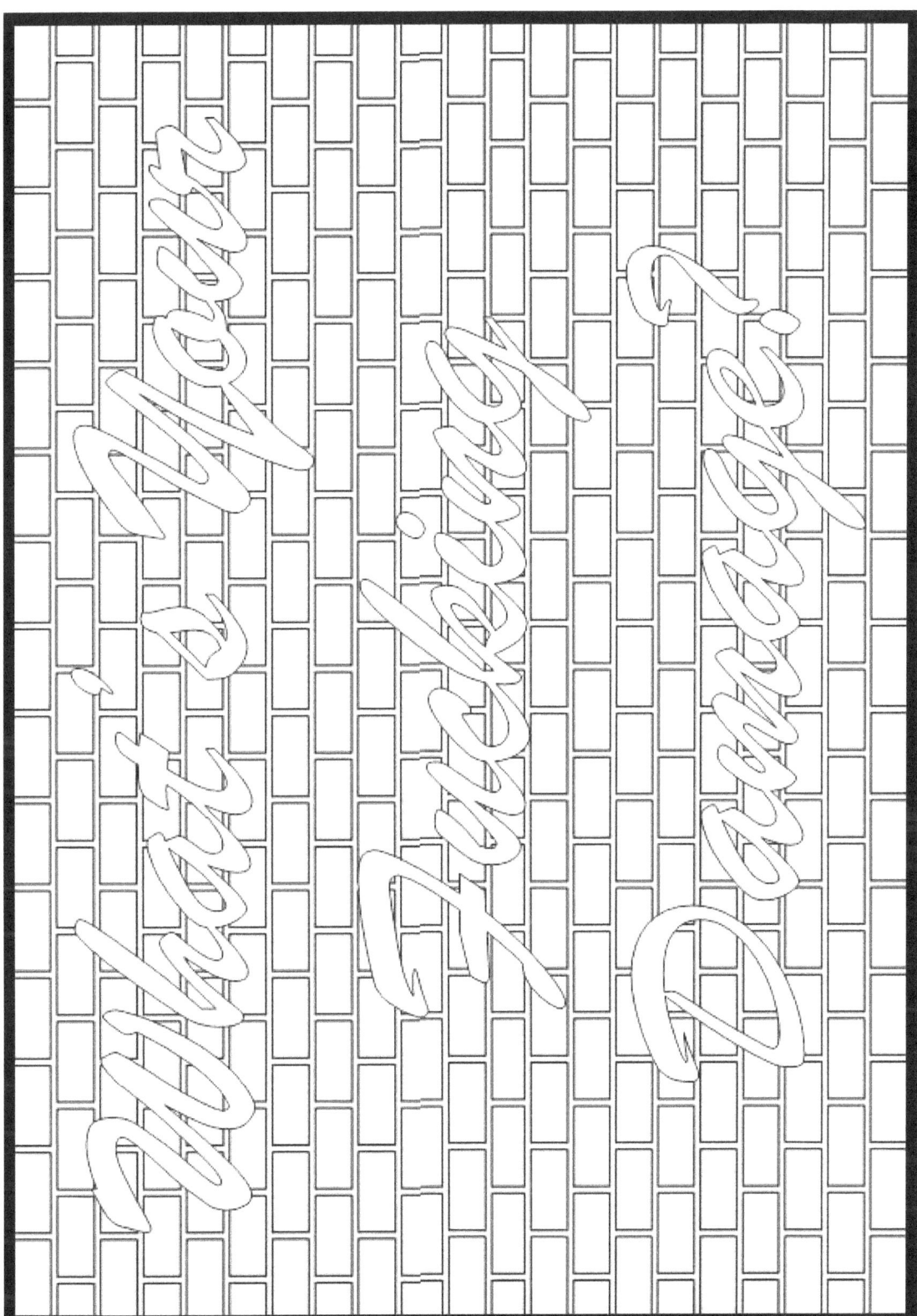

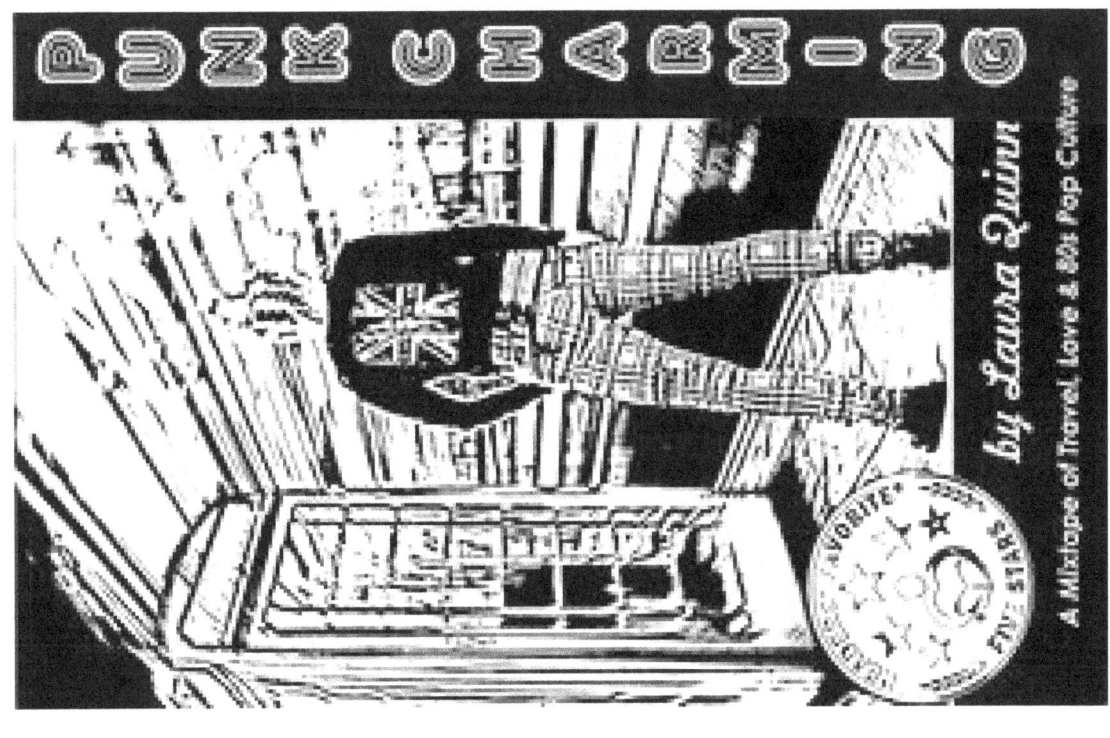

Just Can't Get Enough 80s?

Read *Punk Charming: A Mixtape of Travel, Love & 80s Pop Culture*. Available in paperback and Kindle versions.

"If at any point in your life you wore a rubber bracelet, Duran Duran tee, Fiorenza sweater, Izod with the collar up, a Swatch, or legwarmers, Laura Quinn has a book you are certain to see yourself in. If the success of *Punk Charming* is any indication, her next chapter will be a long one." *Country Magazine*

"Laura Quinn's first novel, *Punk Charming*, is a delightful romp through the 1980s, written with loving detail. The novel is fueled by a soundtrack of Duran Duran, Spandau Ballet, and Wham, along with the spot on period product placement. The net effect is an instant trip back to the fun, edgy mid eighties." *Windy City Reviews*

Visit PunkCharming.net for details.